GREAT GARDENS OF THE
WESTERN WORLD

ENDPAPERS: *Needlework panels, dating from about 1700 from Stoke Edith House, and now on display at Montacute, Somerset*

FRONTISPIECE: *In the garden at Courances, France*

PETER COATS

GREAT GARDENS
OF THE WESTERN WORLD

Introduction by Harold Nicolson

SPRING BOOKS

ISBN: 0 60001649-8

Originally published 1963 by George Weidenfeld & Nicolson Ltd
© 1963 by Peter Coats

This edition published 1968 by
The Hamlyn Publishing Group Ltd
LONDON · NEW YORK · SYDNEY · TORONTO
Hamlyn House, Feltham, Middlesex, England

Printed in Italy by Arnoldo Mondadori Editore Officine Grafiche

Contents

Introduction

By Harold Nicolson

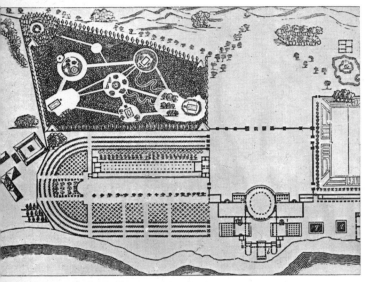

A conjectural plan by Robert Castell of Pliny the Younger's garden overlooking the Bay of Ostia

PETER COATS REMAINS YOUNG and has not ceased to be modest. There is no boasting in this careful book. He does not tell us how, resplendent in a gold and white uniform, he presided over the upkeep of the Lutyens garden at Delhi, directing with the wave of a trowel this stupendous creation, stepping gingerly among the cannas and the golden aureoles. Never since the days of Xenophon has a soldier, and an aide-de-camp to boot, been so precise and efficient a gardener. And now, with equal elegance, he hops from Peterhof to the Villa Taranto, from Winterthur to Bodnant.

The first gardeners known to history were the four daughters of Hesperus, the Evening Star, who owned a garden in the neighbourhood of Agadir, where they cultivated apples of gold. These treasures were guarded by a dragon who never slept. Then there was the gardener of the Pharaohs who is buried in a tomb in the Valley of the Kings, and who is depicted as tying vines to trellis work with thin fussy fingers. At Corfu, King Alcinous, who like most gardeners was not a reticent man, cherished a *hortus inclusus* of four acres. It was enclosed in a hedge and displayed fruit trees in straight rows, some of which had been planted and tended by the King himself. From the paintings at Knossos we can identify the madonna lily, the iris, the crocus and perhaps the rose. Yet the earliest professional gardener, in the Miss Jekyll sense of the term, was Theophrastus, the friend of Plato, who was the first practising horticulturalist to write a book on the subject. He owned a garden of his own near the Lyceum, and was the first man to classify plants into their species. He describes the types of roses known to the ancient Greeks and we note with surprise that in Athens only white and pink roses were in circulation and that there were no purple roses, no yellow, and no red. Theophrastus was buried in one of his own flower beds and instructed his friend to tend the flowers that sprouted from his corpse. Xenophon, the retired general, was another Greek horticulturalist whose main interest was, however, in vegetables and in how to keep garden tools shining and dry. The first scientific study of the art of horticulture is to be found in Pliny's 'Natural History' of which six books are devoted to the science of botany. Pliny suffered badly from asthma, and died gasping during the eruption of Vesuvius. He was a credulous man and believed in winged horses, unicorns, Nereids and Tritons. He tells us that in Roman days flowers were mainly cultivated for garlands and the manufacture of scent; on feast days the standards of the legions were drenched in an epicene unguent manufactured from the *Pallida dalmatica*. The Roman gardens, with their groves of ilex, their statues and terrace walks of myrtle and box must have resembled the stiff gardens of Lucca with their vistas and perspectives, with gravel composed of crushed seashells, *et toujours l'odeur pénétrant des bois*.

The present book, with its excellent illustrations, and Mr Coats' scholarly descriptions, will remind us of the splendid gardens we have ourselves visited in Europe and America, and will recall other gardens of ingenuity and often of beauty, that we have seen in Persia or Japan. It is an error to suppose that the art of garden design is always sharply divided between the 'formal' and the 'natural'. There exist of course many magnificent designs that are 'formal' in their intention and execution, such as those of Versailles, Vaux-le-Vicomte, Villandry, or the admirable little plots that surround the smaller houses at Williamsburg. There also exist, especially in the British Isles, superb 'natural' gardens, such as Bodnant, the Savill Gardens in Windsor Great Park, or the terrace gardens at Tresco Abbey in the Isles of Scilly. Yet there have also been designed many magnificent gardens that are a mixture of formal and natural, such as Bodnant in Wales, the Huntington Gardens in California, the Cypress and Magnolia water gardens near Charleston, or Mr du Pont's splendid succession of gardens at Winterthur.

The essence of garden design, as of all forms of architectural planning, is the alternation of the element of expectation with the element of surprise. There should be present to the mind of the visitor an awareness of the designer's intention; that intention at the same time must be varied, and indeed interrupted, by the unexpected. The main axis of a garden should be indicated, and indeed emphasized, by rectilinear perspectives, by lines of clipped hedges ending in terminals in the form of statues or stone benches. Opening from the main axis there should be smaller enclosed gardens, often constructed round a central pool, and containing some special species or variety of plant. From time to time this variation should be broken and an unexpected feature, such as the superbly surprising Theatre Lawn at Hidcote, be introduced.

I should myself rank Hidcote as the best example of this fusion of expectation with surprise, as the best example that I know of the mingling of the formal and the wild. Yet I question whether in sites of outstanding natural scenery, as at the Villa Taranto, it would be right to introduce too great an element of surprise.

The north façade of the Governor's Palace at Williamsburg through the entrance gates

The elaborate parterre at Villandry

Mysterious shapes of clipped yew at Levens Hall

One of the monsters of Bomarzo

French stone statuary at Bodnant
Gilded statue of Pandora at Peterhof

The tossing mountain peaks that form the background to such scenery are perhaps better contrasted with an orderly formal design, with garden beds planted trimly.

I suspect Mr Coats of sharing my distrust of comic gardens. I do not mean by this the absurdities of garden ornament, such as glass balls and whirligigs, or grotesques like the Mostre di Bomarzo near Viterbo, where monsters of roughly hewn stone gape and belch at the visitor from little kennels of box. Nor do I mean the practical joke gardens of Lucca and La Granja, where the visitor is suddenly doused by a spray of fountain turned on from a concealed tap. Much merriment is caused to courtiers and members of the owner's family by such displays of jocosity. Loud laughter echoes from the laurels. But practical jokes are not for horticulture, which should be the most soothing and sedative of all the arts. I am not so sure that I do not agree with Bacon that topiary also is a form of horticultural merriment. I do not regard Levens Hall gardens as much more than horticultural curiosities; the eye is not rested or soothed by such extravagances. Pediments and finials are excellently rendered, as Bacon pointed out, by well kept topiary, but once the garden designer abandons the architectural for the figurative his design becomes more ingenious than correct. I do not for these reasons regret the decline in our English gardens of the topiarist's art, and, much as I welcome the scraggy semblance of a peacock in a cottage hedge, I do not long for the Laocoön in box.

Henry du Pont, the owner and to a large extent the creator, of the great gardens of Winterthur in Delaware, laid down these rules for the garden designer. The true gardener should plant boldly in large clumps; he should make all possible use of indigenous trees; and he should arrange his colour schemes with meticulous care. It is by such foresight and restraint, practised for nearly a century by the Maclaren family at Bodnant, that superb effects, scenic, architectural and wild, have been achieved. In the hanging woods that form the background of the setting, the Maclarens have, in three generations, staged a remarkable variation of tree foliage, from the darkest to the lightest greens, each bringing out the quality of the other. Then come the formal gardens with their flat ponds, their fountains and their architectural features, such as the entrancing Pin Mill. Then follows the wilder interruptions of rhododendron and azalea, mounting the steep hill-side in ever wilder luxuriance. The wild gardens at Bodnant are not, as at Taranto, overweighted by the mountains behind; they provide a foreground to distance and are not overwhelmed by the magnitude of the distances they fringe.

Of the famous formal gardens illustrated in this book, the most striking to me is that of Peterhof on the Gulf of Finland. The cascades and fountains that form so striking a feature of this hyperborean garden are even superior to the European fountains from which they are imitated, since they are fed by the ice-green water of the Ropsha hills. Nor is the effect of Peterhof diminished by our awareness that this flaunting formal garden was created from a waste of forest and marsh and that beside it are grouped the little Dutch pavilions which Peter the Great constructed, gazing out on the round red eye of the midnight sun.

This sense of cultivation and engineering in remote swamps and forests is conveyed in a totally different way by island gardens, of which the best I know are those of Isola Bella. I have not as yet visited the garden designed by Count Bernadotte at Schloss Mainau on Lake Constance, but I shall go there shortly, reverently holding Mr Coats' book in my hand.

The fact that I have myself derived most enjoyment from the fusing of the natural and the formal in garden design does not in any sense imply that I am unaware of the majesty of formal design and planting. Le Nôtre's superb setting for the terrace, fountains and vistas of Versailles cannot but compel admiration. Yet it is an architectural, rather than a horticultural or landscape masterpiece. So far from providing us with the *hortus inclusus* of classic design, it confronts us with an enormous plateau strewn with fountains and statues, with urns and pyramids. I am aware that this impression of dwarfed nature did not exist in the last decade of Louis XIV's reign when the shrubs and trees that had been planted in full growth had reached their final stature. Yet for several years that great terrace at Versailles must have appeared as a desolated steppe with maggots crawling on the surface. Yet even when the proportion between sky and garden has been readjusted, the impression will remain that the garden in its symmetry is but an extension of the architecture of the palace, stretching wide arms out from the façade of the building to the country beyond. The desire to render the garden an extension of the house itself will always give to the formal garden a sense of artificiality and contrivance. The French, with their taste for proportions, do not mind this disparity; even educated Frenchmen will admire the Tuileries gardens of today, wrongly supposing that they reflect and reinforce the false axis from the Louvre to the Arc de Triomphe, and that formal beds bordered with stiff and desiccated edging plants of green and grey are fine achievements of the gardener's art.

I admit that Versailles, Courances and Villandry are superb achievements of the architectural school of gardening. Yet a garden is intended for the pleasure of its owner and not for ostentation. Nobody could sit with his family on the parterre of Versailles and read the Sunday papers while sipping China tea. Nobody who really cares for flowers can really want them arranged in patterns as if they were carpets from Shiraz or Isphahan. Most civilized people prefer the shade of some dear familiar tree to the opulence of a parterre displaying its pattern under the wide open sky. How infinitely preferable to the vast carpets unrolled in front of Versailles or Vaux-le-Vicomte are

The romantic and theatrical garden of Isola Bella

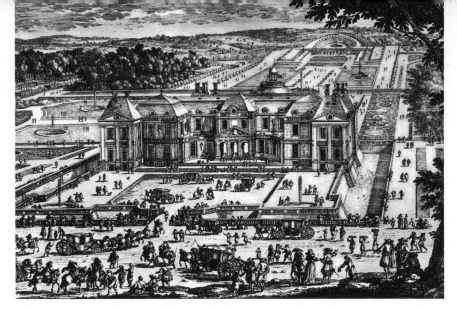

The Entrance to Vaux-le-Vicomte in the seventeenth century

The garden at Tresco Abbey is semi-tropical

the Savill Gardens at Windsor, the variations between the formal and the wild that render the Chatsworth gardens masterpieces of design, the far-flung landscape feature of Stourhead or even the smaller, more intimate, gardens that shine amid the hedgerows of England's green and pleasant land.

It must be recognized, of course, that the softness and intimacy of our English gardens derive mainly from the gentleness and damp of our superb climate. We cannot expect to find in Italy or Spain the moisture that renders our English lawn the basis of our garden design. In other climes the gardener is obliged to fall back on trees and shrubs that can endure prolonged drought and to decorate his gardens with stone benches and statues rather than with clumps of rhododendrons or delphiniums. It is for this reason that Italian gardens in England, as at Hever Castle or Cliveden, always seem chilly, whereas English gardens in Italy tend to appear ill-nourished. A credulous and optimistic gardener, can sometimes, if living in a hill station, convey the momentary impression that the delphinium rather enjoys being at Asolo; yet there hangs a sigh in the air, a sigh for the Ayrshire hills.

The designer must be conscious of the effect he wishes to produce and does not err by seeking to mingle the two simultaneously. At Hidcote, for instance, the vistas and terminals arouse and satisfy our taste for the expected, whereas the small enclosed gardens that diverge from the main axis, respond to our liking for surprise. Thus I regard Bodnant, in its response to these two contrasting expectations, as a masterpiece of design, even as I regard Bagatelle as a triumph of 'the English style'.

The varieties and permutations that can be experimented with between the two terminals of surprise and expectation are numerous and entrancing. Yet the garden designer must be conscious of his objectives and must be clear enough in his intention to be able to avoid giving the impression of fussiness or confusion. He must have his own sketch map clear in his head before he starts to level or plant. He must be sure of the direction in which he wishes his garden to point. He must bear in mind

The entrance to the Hall of the Ambassadors at Alhambra

that in our English climate it is preferable that the main axis should run in a south-westerly direction. He must recognize that the foundations of any good English garden are water, trees, hedges and lawn. He must exercise restraint in combining and contrasting the emotions of surprise and satisfied expectation, and he must bear in mind that plants grow quicker than he may suppose, and that unless he leaves himself ample space, he will find his hedges two feet too close together, and his shrubs squashed up into a bunch. It is preferable to see the earth between your plants and bushes for two whole years than to regret that you disregarded the warnings of your gardening friends and planted too close.

I imagine that Mr Coats would agree that this is good advice and what we most admire in gardens such as Bodnant is the foresight and expert knowledge that have gone to their planting. Gardens, I must again repeat, are intended to bring satisfaction to man by combining in skilled proportions the element of expectation and the element of surprise. Those who read this excellent book with attention and intelligence will agree that the most satisfactory gardens are those which, like Bodnant, combine these two elements and that where the formal is too emphasized, as at Vaux-le-Vicomte, or the wild is allowed to run riot, as in some Scottish gardens, a sense of dissatisfaction is engendered. The principle remains – a wild garden should not become too disordered and a formal garden should not become too stiff.

Splendour or intimacy, which do we prefer? Even in a cottage garden we can, if we possess a sense of proportion, add to its intimacy what Ruskin called 'a sense of infinity'. It is a poor site indeed that offers no vista into the limitless. A book such as this, with its lavish illustrations, the varying samples from every climate, provides us with numerous examples of horticultural skill and endeavour. Taste, unfortunately, cannot be inculcated by any formal precepts, and is the essence of all gardening art. Mr Coats, with his knowledge, his wide experience, and his delicate touch, will help us to realize the meaning of taste.

Stourhead's little replica of the Pantheon

Alhambra GRANADA

Courtyards form the oldest gardens in the world

The entrance to the Court of the Lions, of which the stalactitic decorative scheme of the ceiling has been compared to a petrified grove of palm trees

NEAR GRANADA, IN THE SOUTH OF SPAIN, there is a rocky hill, over which, on leaving the city towards the south, the traveller must pass. It is called 'El Ultimo Suspiro del Moro', the last sigh of the Moor; for it is here, five hundred years ago, that the Moorish King, Boabdil, paused and looked back for the last time on his lost capital, newly conquered by Spain.

The reign of Ferdinand and Isabella (1474–1516) was marked by two great events, the discovery of America and the final expulsion of the Arabs from the Iberian Peninsula. Granada had been in the hands of the Moors for seven hundred years, when, after a ten-year long campaign, it finally surrendered to the armies of the Catholic Sovereigns. The historian Fray Antonio Agapida describes the scene as the Royal procession entered the city: 'The King and Queen moving in the midst' were 'emblazoned with royal magnificence; and as they were in the prime of life, and had now achieved the completion of this glorious conquest, they seemed to represent even more than their wonted majesty. Equal with each other, they were raised far above the rest of the world. They appeared, indeed, more than mortal, and as if sent by heaven for the salvation of Spain.' After a religious service in the principal mosque, newly consecrated as a cathedral, Washington Irving goes on to describe how 'the court ascended to the stately palace of the Alhambra, and entered by the great gate of Justice. The halls, lately occupied by turbaned infidels, now rustled with Christian courtiers, who wandered with eager curiosity over this far-famed palace, admiring its verdant courts and gushing fountains, its halls decorated with elegant arabesques and storied with inscriptions, and the splendour of its gilded and brilliantly painted ceilings.'

We know what a wonderful sight met the eyes of the Spaniards, because, as if by some miracle, the courts and gardens of the Alhambra and the nearby Generalife – in those days they were all one – have changed little from that far-off day to this. The Marquesa de Casa Valdes, the most charming and knowledgeable amateur gardener in Spain, describes the Riadh of the Generalife as being the only garden in Europe which has

RIGHT: *The Court of Lindaraja, known as 'I Ain Dar Aixa', 'Eyes of the Sultana'*

The entrance to the Hall of Abencerrajes from the Court of the Lions

kept its original fourteenth-century lines, 'just as the Arabs first traced them'. The Marquesa, in her admirable description of the Alhambra and Generalife, goes on to say:

To be able to understand southern gardens, it is necessary to know the climate and the mentality of the inhabitants. In Western Europe, all parks, gardens and lay-outs that surround large and important mansions of the seventeenth and eighteenth centuries, were designed to enhance their splendour, and as a sequence to these palaces. The mode of living of the period required it. Parties and fêtes were celebrated and necessitated terraces and gardens on the grand scale as an appropriate setting. We have examples of similar estates in the Royal Palaces of La Granja and Aranjuez, influenced by Italian and French models. But Arab gardens, whose origin is Persia, from which country they have received a direct influence, were planned and conceived for the retired mode of living of only a small number of inhabitants, for a sedentary and contemplative existence. The complex and refined art of the Moor is very far removed from our mentality and our time. To enable us to understand it, we would have to call to mind those Orientals who created beauty for the pleasure of slowly contemplating it without regard for the passage of time. The gardens of Granada to this day have kept their characteristic structure of court and garden which is typical of the mode of life of southern Spain.

These courts or patios, after centuries of experiment in which their traditional form was established, are the result of a perfect adaptation to the soil and climate of the South. During the heat of the summer, those who dwell in them seek coolness within the four walls of their home. It is therefore in Spain, more than in any other country, that the 'patio', common to all Mediterranean cultures, has kept its tradition, and it expresses to this day the mode and daily life of its inhabitants.

The influence of the patio is so great that one can safely say that the Granada garden is composed of a series of green chambers, where the principal role is played by the murmur of the water and by the light which varies according to the hour of the day, and where the highest degree of beauty is reached on nights of full moon, heavy with the scented atmosphere of jasmine and of orange blossom.

A series of courtyards, sky-ceiled and open to the cool breezes which blow from the snowy Sierra Nevada, today greets the visitor to the Alhambra. Each of its courtyards has its own character, just as in the days of the Abencerrajes each had its own purpose. But, in each, water plays the important role. The Arabs, six hundred years ago, brought water to the Alhambra by an elaborate system of reservoirs and canals which is still in use today. In the gardens of Granada, water is everywhere, in fountains, pools, running in rivulets through tiny canals which find their way through the actual rooms of the palace. An Arab poet has said, 'Water is the music of the Alhambra'.

One of the largest pools in the Alhambra is in the Court of Comares, the court of the Ambassadors. According to an Arab inscription on the frieze of the northern porch, 'The Sultan, Muhammad V, finished the famous construction of his Palace about the year 1369'. On either side of the pool, which has fountains at both ends, are neatly-tailored hedges of myrtle, the sombre green of the hedge setting off the cool whiteness of the marble. It was by the Court of Comares that the Arab Kings had their throne room, and from here they could contemplate a distant view of Granada, framed in its graceful windows.

The most famous courtyard of the Alhambra is the Court of the Lions, where Mohammedan art surely reaches its peak of beauty. Of it, Professor Francisco Prieto Moreno writes: 'The stalactite ornamentation of the ceilings brings to our mind the structure and erection of a royal tent, of perfect proportions, which has been placed in a petrified forest of palm trees, and at whose feet a spring would flow. This theory, which may seem exaggerated, symbolizes the innate tendency of the Arab to introduce nature into the rich forms of architecture, result of the refinement created by the decadence and softness due to the sedentary life the Arab led in the centuries preceding the conquest of Granada.

The Court of the Lions is now neatly gravelled over, but in the days of the Arab kingdom it was surely planted with trees,

The Patio of the Myrtles (de los Arrayanes) in 1842, showing the rich Moorish decoration

17

ALHAMBRA

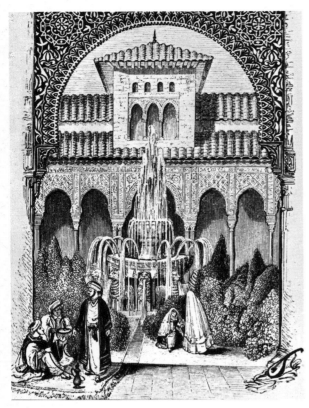

The Court of the Lions in the days of the Moorish kings

The harmless looking lions supporting the fountain date from the tenth century

filled with flowers and herbs in pots, an intimate *Hortus inclusus* with air heavy from the scent of orange flowers and the brisk tang of pot herbs, and continually refreshed by the sound of falling water from the twelve-sided Lion fountain which bears, on one of its panels, the almost ridiculous inscription which imagines what the ferocity of the lions would have been, had not respect for the Calif held them in check. Six tamer, more cuddly-looking lions, would be hard to find.

Another courtyard of the Alhambra is the Patio of the Lindaraja, whose miradors are now no longer open to the view, since King Charles V blocked it with Renaissance additions. It was here that the American writer, Washington Irving, lodged in the last century. This patio, in Arab days, lay with an open prospect towards the fortress of the Albaicin on one side and a mirador, or balcony, called *I Ain Dar Aixa*, or 'Eyes of the Sultana', on the other. Though today the patio of the Lindaraja is dark, secret and enclosed, it seems to distill the very essence of the spirit of the Alhambra, as its fountains drip away the centuries.

Leaving the Alhambra, the visitor climbs a hillside, dark and cool with the shade of trees and serenaded at night by innumerable nightingales, towards the Generalife. Of it, the Marquesa de Casa Valdes has written:

In their desire to enjoy greater seclusion and to come closer to nature, the Princes of Granada built a series of Palaces, high on the cliff, amid the woodlands on the prolongation towards the east of the Sabika, or red hill. Of all these palaces which overlooked the Alhambra, only the Generalife remains, situated to the north-east and at a short distance from the Alhambra. Its creation was made possible, thanks to the *acequia*, or Royal Canal, a stream canalized by the Arabs which passes through the garden of the Generalife and afterwards waters the Alhambra with its fountains and gardens.

As distinct from the Alhambra, where the architecture controls the vegetation amid its walls and marbles, the charm of the Generalife lies in its having kept the character of a simple country-house, composed of two small pavilions, placed opposite one another with the main garden between them. These pavilions are surrounded and nearly hidden by the woods which adjoin the Generalife, and the garden in the time of the Arabs was a modest orchard.

The magnificent panorama unfolded from the Generalife, with the towers of the Alhambra silhouetted against the fertile valley of Granada, seems to lose itself in space. The majestic mountains of the Sierra Nevada, amongst the loftiest in Spain and always snow-capped, detach themselves from the intense blue of the sky, making this spot one of the most spectacular in the world.

There are different interpretations of the word 'Generalife', but according to the historian Hernando de Baeza, it means 'the most lofty orchard, without rival', which is surely apt.

The traveller, Andrea Navaggiero, who visited the Generalife thirty-four years after the fall of Granada in 1522, has left a description of it which is full of admiration, and writes of its

RIGHT: *The Patio de la Riadh. Brimming flower beds border the canal with its many-jetted fountains*

The legend-haunted Sultana's cypress in the Court of the Sultana is said to be over a thousand years old

many patios and canals bordered with myrtle and oranges. He also adds that its most interesting feature, then as now, is the water staircase, of which the Marquesa writes:

> The balustrade consists of masonry walls hollowed out on the top to form a canal of concave Arab tiles along which the waters glide swiftly. This staircase is covered with a dense canopy of laurel and other evergreens through whose foliage the sunbeams play upon the water as it runs through the balustrade and leaps in the fountains. Amidst the different sections of these gardens, subject to variation and ephemeral as they all are, this simple staircase provides the most interesting feature, besides being the most authentic object in the Generalife. It can safely be asserted that it has kept its original form from the Arab period.

That is, before the year 1319, when, according to the inscriptions that surround the arches, the decoration was renovated.

But it is the Garden of the Riadh which is the heart of the Generalife. It measures forty metres long by thirteen metres wide, and down its centre, between arching fountains (later but highly effective additions) and flowers and fruit trees, runs a canal of water. At either end are exquisite scalloped alabaster basins. The whole concept typifies the peak of Arab gardening art. The design of the fountains and their marble basins recall the gardens of the East, the Taj Mahal and the fabulous gardens of Kashmir.

On one side of the Riadh is a range of arches of great beauty which overlook, as from an eagle's eyrie, the rich *vega* of Granada, emerald green in spring, burnished gold in summer. It is this arcade which gives the garden all its charm. 'Thanks to it', says the Marquesa, 'the reduced size which would have been darkened by a wall or a cypress hedge, is lit up with an airy luminosity which filters through the arches without altering the atmosphere of mystery and seclusion.' Above the Riadh, lies the romantic patio of the Sultana's cypress, of which an ancient cypress is the *genius loci*. This tree, which is many hundred years old, is said to have been the meeting place of a Sultana Queen and an Abencerraje knight. Above this patio lie more gardens, terraced and arranged in the Renaissance style, as parterres of clipped box, with carved stone fountains.

But though all the gardens of the Generalife and the Alhambra, even the modern addition through which the visitor passes on arrival, have great beauty, in thinking of it afterwards, it will be to the Garden of the Riadh that his thoughts will surely fly. It is this garden which provides all the elements of Arab garden design: and, as the Marquesa has written:

> ... the porch, the small basins, the canal, the water-jets that border it, the vegetation, and the distant vision of the landscape framed by the balconies at the back of the pavilion and its lateral arcaded gallery from whence the massive silhouette of the Alhambra can be seen. All this together resembles a marvellous symphonic poem which reveals to us the ecstatic qualities of the Islamic soul.

RIGHT: *Bold groups of Arum lilies grow in the canal which runs the length of the newly planted garden which leads to the Generalife*

La Gamberaia NEAR FLORENCE

An Italian garden in the classic manner

ONE GARDEN BEFORE ALL OTHERS in the region of Florence has retained the atmosphere of the *Settecento*, and that is La Gamberaia. For many years the villa was used as a simple guesthouse, and this *dégringolade* doubtless saved its garden plan from drastic change. The parterres were used to grow cabbages and corn rather than profitless flowers, and there was no money to spare for nineteenth-century improvements. Italy is a country, like Japan, where small areas of land are put to fullest use, and at Gamberaia today the visitor can see how, on a relatively small scale, a spectacular effort was achieved by its original architects. The Villa lies outside Settignano and commands the green, umbrageous valley of the Arno.

The garden comprises, with ease and no feeling of overcrowding in its small area, most of the amenities of the classic Italian garden, as well as one which is unusual – the long sweep of mown grass which runs the length of the formal garden; a lawn anywhere in Italy is unusual, and this one is all the more so by reason of its size. Italian garden planners admired greensward, but used it only as a luxury which demanded constant watering and maintenance. Expanses of turf were never taken for granted, as they are in cooler, damper climates. They were always luxuries, and usually, if planted at all, placed near the house, where their refreshing green could be constantly admired.

Other delights of the garden at Gamberaia include high, tonsured hedges of yew for shade, four formal *pièces d'eau* to reflect the Tuscan sky (these, the hedges and pools, are later but entirely satisfactory additions to the garden), and, opposite the main entrance to the Villa, a tiny grotto-garden, with fern-grown fountain, pebble-work walls and a pair of bumpkin lovers, ogling each other from their niches of rusticated stone.

The gardens at the Gamberaia (the word, unexpectedly enough, means 'Shrimpery') are an example of the importance in garden-planning of the sub-division of spaces. Of this, Miss Edith Wharton in her *Italian Villas* wisely wrote:

Whereas the modern gardener's one idea of producing an effect of space is to annihilate his boundaries, and not only to merge into one

Asymmetrical fenestration and conical yew-trees are reflected in the pools

LEFT: '*A bumpkin lover*' *in the grotto garden*

23

another the necessary divisions of the garden, but also to blend this vague whole with the landscape, the old garden-architect proceeded on the opposite principle, arguing that, as the garden is but the prolongation of the house, and as a house containing a single huge room would be less interesting and less serviceable than one divided according to the varied requirements of its inmates, so a garden which is merely one huge outdoor room is also less interesting and less serviceable than one which has its logical divisions.

The recent history of Gamberaia is full of incident. It was rescued from its unworthy existence as a boarding house by Princess Jeanne Ghika, who, in the words of her niece, Princess Marthe Bibesco, 'was rich, beautiful and hated men and mankind'. But the Princess certainly lavished her love on the Gamberaia, and devotedly restored and replanted the garden with great taste. Not everyone at the time thought so, but now that her hedges have reached their full, rich maturity, few would criticize her imagination and foresight. In the last war, the villa was successively occupied by the German Gestapo and blown up by the Allies, and then occupied by the Allies and blown up by the Germans. It was used as a storehouse for Italian military maps, and the final conflagration was such that it burned for a whole week. It was almost an empty shell when Doctor Marcello Marchi bought it and once more restored it. The gardens, though naturally neglected during the war, suffered little damage. Miraculously, Princess Ghika's yew hedges survived, and today their high green arches frame a view over the Arno valley as lovely as any in Italy.

A harpist in stucco, in a setting of rustic stone

TOP LEFT: *The Villa, built in 1610, shows little baroque influence . . . but is wholly Tuscan in its sober architecture*

'On a small scale, a spectacular effect was achieved'

LEFT: *The unusual feature of the garden at Gamberaia – the Great Lawn*

Planning and plant-form at Gamberaia

The west façade through a filigree of roses
A seventeenth-century print of the Villa Gamberaia and its environs

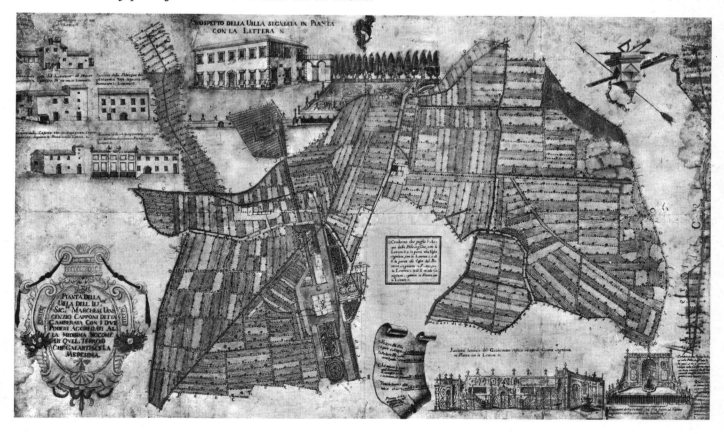

LEFT: *Framed in an arch of yew, the plastic shapes of topiary at Gamberaia*

Kasteel Twickel HOLLAND

Parterres round a moated Dutch castle

The castle in 1729

ONE EVENING IN JUNE 1727 a cavalcade of coaches crossed the bridge over the moat of Kasteel Twickel. From the most splendid of the equipages emerged a small, fat old gentleman, with popping, pale blue eyes and pendant cheeks. King George I of England was travelling to Hanover and was dining with Count Twickel on the way. After a large dinner, at which the King ate a quantity of peaches and grapes, he complained of indigestion. Next day, as his coach rolled up to his brother's palace at Osnabrück, he was found in it, dead, as a result of a stroke. Thus briefly history touched Twickel; and then left it to drowse once more.

Kasteel Twickel was built in the fourteenth century by Herman van Twickel, and altered and enlarged through the centuries. It took its present form in 1706 when the back wing was added by Jacob van Wassenaar, and the elaborately carved *wapensteen* was hoisted into place above the front door. This is flanked on either side by a naked Adam and Eve in stone, unkindly placed aloft on high pillars, to shiver in every gust of the east wind which blows from the nearby German frontier.

The garden at Twickel was laid out soon after. The elaborate orangery certainly existed in 1770, as can be seen in a print of that date. The deer park – two hundred years later – is still the home of 'dappled fools'. The present owner, Baroness van

RIGHT: *Spring lays a carpet of colour in the informal garden at Twickel*

Sculptured box makes a baroque pattern by the side of the moat

Heeckeren van Twickel, whose late husband descended from the original builder of the Kasteel, has of recent years brought the garden to perfection. Its essentially Dutch character has been preserved – the courtyard, the drawbridges, the trim parterres, cut in the shaven lawns. But it is the moat, afloat with water lilies and curtained with roses, which most reflects the garden at Twickel, and its cool water seems to refresh and animate the scene.

Baroness van Heeckeren, though over eighty, is a dedicated gardener, and to the original eighteenth-century scheme at Twickel has added more gardens of her own. The rose garden was planted before the First World War and was designed by Rabjohn, the famous gardener from Welbeck Abbey. The Baroness herself designed the rock garden and the attractive wavy-edged border, sheltered by high trees, in which grow herbaceous plants and lilies. So active is she, that when her family presented her on her birthday with a thatched summer-house, their doubt was whether the Baroness would ever spare time from her gardening chores to sit in it.

A lion glaring across a box parterre. The castle door has changed little since 1729

LEFT: *A Bonsai, a hundred or more years old: a Japanese miniature tree, the word coming from bon, a pot, and sai, a plant*

31

Earlshall SCOTLAND

A topiary garden in the kingdom of Fife

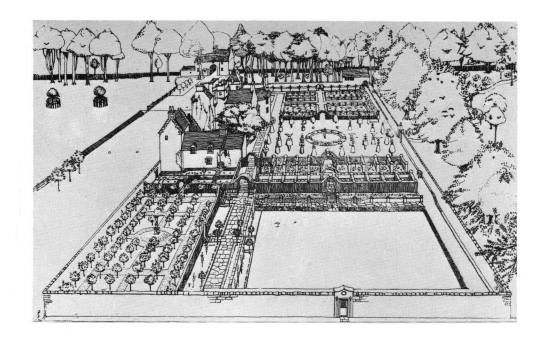

The garden as projected in 1900, from H. Inigo Triggs book 'Formal Gardens in England and Scotland'

'SCOTLAND WAS ANYTHING BUT BONNY five hundred years ago.' Thus the author of this book once wrote in an essay on Scottish gardens, and he went on to say: 'The heather and the mountains were there, it is true, but there were few trees, few flowers, and in a country which was continually at war with England or itself – certainly no gardens.' The old pre-historic forests had been cut down for fuel, what flowers there were were wild, and houses were either fortresses or hovels. The climate, too, had a strange reputation. Few plants, apparently, could survive it, and those that could, were freakish, to say the least. Aenaeas Piccolomini, afterwards Pope Pius II, who toured Scotland in the reign of King James I (1394–1437), mentions a pear-bush that produced fruit in the shape of geese, which, when ripe, would drop off and fly away. He also noted the complete lack of trees, and general bleakness of the countryside, which, a hundred years later, were to depress the French followers of Mary Queen of Scots. Nor were vegetables cultivated to any extent: the Scots did not like them, and laughed at the Grant clan who ate them – the 'soft kail-eating Grants'. The reputation of Scotland's climate persisted. In the seventeenth century, Fynes Morison wrote: 'In the Northerne Parts of England they have small pleasantnesse . . . or abundance of fruit and flower, so in Scotland they must have lesse, or none at all.' Even Doctor

LEFT: *The bright flower cups of early peonies lighten a corner of the garden already rich with the foliage of spring*

The giant chessmen in yew were moved when already fully grown

A path of diagonally laid brick crosses one of informal paving in the kitchen garden

Johnson, who should have known better, and who admittedly was against Scotland generally, described the climate as so bad that the Scots had to grow barley under glass.

They were all, of course, quite wrong. Scotland has as good a gardening climate as England: and in the west, where the coast is washed by the comforting Gulf Stream, the climate is better. Even on the east coast, where the wind can blow briskly enough, the sun shines more consistently than in many parts of England. Fife, where the garden we describe in this chapter lies, is noted for its low rainfall and long sunshine days.

To tell the story of Earlshall from the start, we must go back to 1538 when King James V of Scotland met his French bride, Mary of Guise, at nearby St Andrews: a few days later they were married in Edinburgh. For Scotland the marriage was unfortunate: it aligned the country definitely with France; it ended all hopes of the essential alliance with England; and it threatened the Reformed Kirk. The only child of the union was the ill-starred Mary Queen of Scots. James died four years after his wedding day, Mary was Queen at the age of one week, and Scotland was to see no peace for fifty years. The country was to have little time for house-building, far less for garden planting, for half a century.

However, the castle of Earlshall had been completed just in time. Its builder was Sir William Bruce, a member of the ancient family which had given several kings to Scotland. In the troubles that followed King James' death the castle escaped the wars, which was fortunate, as its battlements were more decorative than defensive and its high walls were designed to withstand robbers and feuding neighbours more than the artillery of an army. The Bruces, siding now with one faction, now with another, survived the disorders of the Reformation and the Regency of Mary of Guise, and after the girl-queen Mary returned to Scotland in 1561 she came hawking in the Earlshall woods, where, then as now, there was a famous heronry. In 1580, Earlshall was lived in by Sir William's grandson, Alexander: his initials, and those of his wife Euphame Leslie, appear over the carved fireplace in the great hall of the castle.

Houses, whether castles or not, in sixteenth-century Scotland, were far from luxurious: they were refuges from the weather and unfriendly neighbours, they were storehouses for food and game. In them life was simple and rough: men spent their life outdoors and would 'Liefer hear the lark sing than the mouse squeak'. But Lady Bruce, though she probably had but simple furniture to put in it, had in her newly furnished home one most remarkable room. Although our purpose in this chapter is to describe the garden at Earlshall, mention must be made of the gallery which lies in an upper part of the house – a surprising room over fifty feet long, painted most elaborately in an all-over pattern of scrolls, strapwork, stylized flowers, foliage and different shaped panels, each with a decorative device, coat of arms or admonitory injunction. Here are depicted such unexpected animals as the Shoe Lyon, the Musk Ket and the Mouse of Arabia, interspaced with pieces of worldly wisdom such as 'A nice wyf and a back doore oft makyth a rich man poore', the meaning of which can be interpreted in several ways.

The interior of Earlshall was the subject of a masterly reconstruction by that great Scottish architect Sir Robert Lorimer (1864–1929) in the first years of the century: but the exterior is much as it was in the days of Sir Alexander. Its corbel-work, craw-stepped gables, and grey stone walls, complete with defensive bartizan and towering chimneys against the hurrying clouds of the Fifeshire sky, make a most romantic background for the garden.

Mr and Mrs Arthur Purvis bought Earlshall in 1926 and at once set about replanting the garden, which had been laid out to its present plan by Sir Robert Lorimer thirty years before. It was Sir Robert who introduced the many clipped-yew 'chessmen', which were successfully transplanted from a derelict garden near Edinburgh in 1895, and which today give the garden such character.

The visitor to the garden at Earlshall is greeted on arrival by a rugged carpet of paving stones, a typical Lorimer fancy, laid in a semi-formal pattern. Passing through a shady courtyard he finds the garden stretched before him; and if it is a sunny evening, the best of all times of the day to see a garden, the peacocks and pepper pots of meticulously clipped yew cast odd shadows on the lawn: yew delights in the light sandy soil of Fife. In flower beds walled with evergreens, flowers glow in the evening light, and everywhere in the garden are to be seen the thoughtful touches which give a garden character: one old stone wall is buttressed with blocks of yew, interspersed with

A cobbled floor of a courtyard

silver leaved *senecio*, a formal planting which looks well all the year through. There are several good examples of attractive paving at Earlshall, and the contrast of grey dressed stone and pebblework is in several places repeated. The walls and yew hedges provide shelter for many shrubs which are considered delicate further south in the British Isles, such as *Parrotia persica* with blazing leaves in autumn, the unusual blue daisy-flowered *Microglossa albescens*, the shrubby starwort and the white flowered *carpenteria* of which each flower has a boss of golden stamens.

Many of the old roses are grown at Earlshall and show their flowers to perfection against the old walls and hedges; roses like the white splashed with purple, *Variegata di Bologna*, *William Lobb*, the well named snowy *Boule de Neige*, and Mrs Purvis' special favourite, *Fritz Nobis*.

Over the garden door at Earlshall is carved a quotation from *As You Like It:* 'Here shall ye see no enemy but winter and rough weather.' But though spring comes late to Scottish gardens, summer lingers.

Initials, dating from the sixteenth century, on the gallery ceiling

'Such unexpected animals as the Shoe Lyon'
This can be interpreted in several different ways

Earlshall as it is today . . .

. . . and as it was before its restoration

Aranjuez NEAR MADRID

The gardens of the kings of Spain

Philip II of Spain, who planted the garden at Aranjuez and brought many of the trees for it from England

AS EXOTIC IN SPAIN AS A GROVE OF banyan trees would be at Bournemouth, the English elms of Aranjuez are still one of the minor wonders of the area near Madrid. A king of England planted them, Philip II, husband of Mary Tudor, and recognized as monarch of England by Parliament in 1554. He had seen elm trees when he journeyed there to marry the Queen and had imported them into Spain, so it is probable that the plans for the Armada, and the 'Enterprise of England' were discussed under the shadow of these most English of trees.

The green *vega* at Aranjuez, for many centuries the country retreat of the Spanish kings, presents an oasis of cool verdure in the brown desert of the countryside thirty miles south of Madrid. Shaded by Philip's elms, and watered by both the Rivers Tagus and Xarama, which meet almost in the palace gardens, the gardens of Aranjuez remain fresh throughout the most torrid Spanish summer. H. V. Morton has written:

> Castilians who have never travelled, believe that Aranjuez is the lushest spot on this planet and a faithful replica of the earthly paradise. It is, in effect, a little corner of France beside the Tagus. Here the Bourbons erected a palace in imitation of Versailles, with grottoes and fountains, with endless avenues and shady places, where it seems that the music of the last *fête champêtre* has only just died away; indeed, one might fancy that footmen are only just packing up the remains of cold partridge, and the musicians putting away their flutes.

And it is true that the avenues and bosquets of Aranjuez have not changed greatly since the days of Philip IV.

The palace is approached through a grandiose formal garden planted with thousands of red roses round a vast and monumental fountain, the centre of which is a white marble piece of statuary representing the Labours of Hercules. Beyond that lies a neat parterre with the arms of Spain clipped in box lying like a rich carpet before the north façade of the palace. But it is the gardens to the west of the palace which linger in the memory. They are situated on an island, washed on either side by the waters of the Xarama River and set with avenues and enfilades of Philip's elms. These are the Jardines de l'Isla which so impressed

RIGHT: *In the foreground, a plant of acanthus, inspiration of architects since classic times: beyond, the arms of Spain in clipped box*

ARANJUEZ

A rose-crowned sphinx in a leafy setting

The rivers Xarama and Tagus meet under the palace walls

Lady Fanshaw, wife of Charles II's Ambassador to Spain:

We went privately to see Aranjuez, which was most part of it built by Philip the Second, husband to Queen Mary of England. There are the highest trees, and grow up the evenest, that ever I saw; many of them are bored through with pipes for water to ascend and to fall from the top down one against another, and likewise there are many fountains in the side of this walk, and the longest walks of elms I ever saw in my life. The park is well stored with English oaks and elms, and deer; and the Tagus makes it an island. The gardens are vastly large, with the most fountains, and the best that ever I saw in my life.

Water no longer falls from the tops of the trees, but the sound of water is all about the island gardens, splashing from the many fountains and murmuring as the twin rivers flow slowly by. The soil at Aranjuez is rich and fertile and is famous for strawberries and asparagus. In 1555 the first Spanish botanic gardens, in which medicinal herbs were studied and cultivated, was planted at Aranjuez, following the dedication by Dr Laguna of his translation of Dioscorides to Philip II. In it the doctor suggests that such a botanical garden would not only teach His Majesty's subjects much they needed to know about *la disciplina herbaria*, but would doubtless benefit the King's health as well.

The gardens of Aranjuez have witnessed endless political and court intrigues. From the days of Philip II onwards their shade has been sought by lovers for assignations, and by politicians for secret meetings. Some of the lovers who have met under their branches were the one-eyed but fascinating Princess of Eboli and Antonio Perez. Here courtiers have loitered seeking to attract the King's eye for some special petition. Philip's elms have heard all their secrets, and the waters of the Xarama and the Tagus have carried them all silently away. The first scene of Schiller's dark tragedy *Don Carlos* is laid in the gardens of Aranjuez. Let the famous opening words of his play be the last of this chapter:

Die schönen Tage in Aranjuez
Sind nun zu ende.

RIGHT: *Foliage and marble figures create the atmosphere of Aranjuez*

The fountains and the flowing river refresh the green glades of Aranjuez

A bridge from the palace leads to the Jardines de l'Isla

The water of the Xarama washes the palace walls

*The Fuente de Hercules at the
entrance to the palace gardens*

Philip's elms still shade the avenues of Aranjuez, of which the largest is called the 'Salon de los Reyes Católicos'

Villandry INDRE-ET-LOIRE

A spectacular recreation of a Renaissance garden

The château below the cloudy sky of Touraine beyond a close-shorn hedge of hornbeam

CHARLES VIII OF FRANCE, campaigning in Italy in 1495, wrote home from Naples to his cousin Pierre de Bourbon: 'You cannot believe what beautiful gardens I have seen in this town: for, on my word, it seems as though only Adam and Eve were wanting to make an earthly paradise, so full are they of rare and beautiful things.' His enterprise – it was to seize the throne of Naples – yielded few gains for France politically: Charles failed in his attempt on the Neapolitan Crown and returned to France with a sadly diminished army. Tangible gains of the campaign seemed few, and yet, although he probably did not realize it, the booty he brought home with him was inestimable: the ideas which were to inspire the French Renaissance. Not only that: he brought back, too, the artists to carry them out. Twenty-two of them were housed in his favourite castle of Amboise, which he aimed to make, with its garden, the fairest in France. His premature death, two years later, did not affect the growth of the plant, the seeds of which he had sown. His successor Louis XII, and France's next King, the amorous and belligerent François I, carried on the work. The architectural achievements of the following century and the development of French garden design, are immortalized in a unique set of engravings by the architect Jacques Androuet du Cerceau (1515–84). These engravings, with their crystal line, offer the clearest picture of the

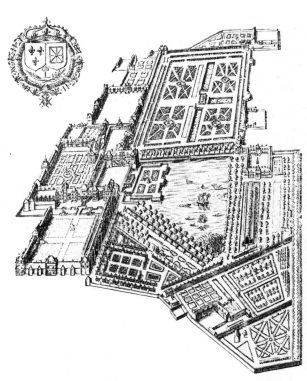

An engraving by Jacques Androuet du Cerceau (1515–1584) of the garden plan of Fontainebleau. Du Cerceau's drawings inspired much of the reconstruction of the garden at Villandry

LEFT: *The elaborate parterre lies beneath the terrace wall*

The pattern is a complex one

building activities of this robust and burgeoning period, when the royalty and nobility of France seemed inspired by the heart-warming breeze of the Renaissance.

King Charles's campaign in Italy, and the stories he and his followers told of the marvels they had seen there, encouraged many young Frenchmen to venture south over the Alps, to taste the heady wine of Italy and its architectural splendours, both classic and of the day. But though they drank deep of the offered cup, and learned much, the Frenchmen kept their heads, and preserved a praiseworthy independence and conservatism, either on account of their innate chauvinism or because they realized the architecture of Italy was not ideally suited to their own cooler climate. Not for them the pavilions open to every breeze and the airy loggias of the South: and however much Italian ideas of decoration might be valued indoors, exteriors in France, though embellished and refined, remained, to begin with, largely unaltered. Castles, in the main, retained their mediaeval plan, and if rebuilt, were rebuilt on the original foundations: their moats were usually retained, leaving little scope for gardens on the Italian scale, with formal lay-outs centering on the castle itself. The new French gardens had to be planned wherever there was room for them, often, and the Château de Villandry is an example, at an oblique angle to the house.

Although no Du Cerceau engraving exists of Villandry as it originally was, the designs for Fontainebleau, Charleval and Verneuil all helped to inspire the reconstruction of the gardens – one of the most elaborate recreations of a garden ever to have been attempted.

The Château of Villandry and its garden

The Château de Villandry lies a few miles west of Tours, between the rivers Cher and Loire, and is, thanks to the masterly reconstruction of the garden, the only one of the fabled châteaux of the Loire which can be seen in its contemporary garden framework. Two of the other great French châteaux included in this book, Vaux-le-Vicomte and Versailles, are at least a hundred years later.

The reconstructed garden at Villandry, with its subtle relationship between architectural and garden plan, enables us to evaluate the French good-sense and logic which controlled their enthusiasm for the early intoxication of the Renaissance. The late Dr Carvallo himself, the re-creator of the garden of Villandry, seems to have been impressed by these qualities, for he once wrote:

> What most strikes the visitor at first sight is the orderliness of the surroundings of the house. The *basse-cour* is low, the forecourt somewhat raised, the court of honour yet higher. Owner, passer-by, and beasts are each set in their place, yet related and without possibility of confusion. This disposition is typical of French domestic planning as originally conceived by the Benedictines and reflected in all seigneurial establishments till the end of the eighteenth century. Thereafter, however, such ordered planning was abandoned, and at Villandry, as at Versailles, the nineteenth century destroyed the levels distinguishing the functional purpose of each court, substituting a single inclined plane: so that men and creatures insensibly slid in the direction of the stables, while animals, without the least effort, could stray into the drawing-room. This destruction of the domestic hierarchy was due to the influence of English and German philosophers who, by their inordinate love of nature and excessively egalitarian conception of the world, reduced man to the status of animals.

A stone watch dog by the south lodge

'Swans Way' . . . *the moat from the tower*

The spectacular potager with its many rose wreathed arbours
' One of the most elaborate recreations of a garden ever to have been attempted '

The walls of the château rise sheer from the moat
The colour and pattern of the unique potager

The chateau itself was built by Jean Lebreton, a Minister of François I, in the first half of the sixteenth century. It was built on the foundations of the ancient fortress of Colombier of which the high castellated south-west corner and two sides of the moat survive. The present structure fills three sides of a square, round a courtyard entered by means of a drawbridge. The elegantly fenestrated and neatly string-coursed garden façade, surmounted by the high pitched roof and mansard windows, mirrors itself in the newly filled moat, from which the walls of the château rise. Dr Carvallo was of the opinion that the architects of the early Renaissance prided themselves on the extra check on the quality of their elevations provided by the retention of the mediaeval moat: this, by reflecting the façade, accentuated the perfection of its lines, in the same way as a portrait painter will test the likeness he has achieved by holding a looking-glass to his picture. In the seventeenth and eighteenth centuries such subtleties were overlooked, and the façades of châteaux like Azay-le-Rideau and Chambord lost much by being deprived of water. Villandry gains immeasurably from its refilled moat.

It is the west façade of the château which overlooks the garden, one of the most remarkable in Europe. The original Renaissance garden was obliterated in the nineteenth century, though enough of its original structure – terrace walls, steps, and paved paths – survived to facilitate Dr Carvallo's work of reconstruction. The garden today presents twelve acres of intricate pattern which might seem overwhelming and tedious, were it not for the difference in levels which characterizes it. The enormous area is divided into four tiers: the two uppermost are carved from the slight hill lying to the north of the château; the second of these two upper tiers is on the same level as, and connects with, the top floor of the château itself. This offers a raised walk round two sides of the whole garden. The third tier is on the same level as the main floor, and comprises the pleasure garden and *potager*. The fourth lies level with the moat which now once more laves the lower stonework of the château on its southern front. Thus, full advantage has been taken of the contours of the site, and variety and zest given to what otherwise might have appeared a bewildering expanse of geometrical parterres. Mr Christopher Hussey has written:

As it is, the whole recalls the idea of the hanging gardens of Semiramis which fascinated other Renaissance aesthetes besides Sir Thomas Browne. Aesthetically this interplay of planes serves the purpose of providing that feeling of contrast which the English landscape gardeners achieved by reproducing pictorial effects in their compositions. Similarly the elements of texture and colour, provided in the English scheme by lawn and natural vegetation, is here formalized as geometrical parterres; and that of water, instead of simulating a natural lake or brook, as rectilinear canals and fountains. Shade, as a physical requirement, is afforded in the most logical way by pleached alleys of limes or vine pergolas following the main divisions and presenting exactly the appearance of those galleries described by Francis

Bacon and other contemporaries, in English Tudor gardens.

The pleasure-grounds and vegetable gardens at Villandry have extraordinary charm. The former, with their close-set parterres of box-edged beds, geometrically planned and intimately interwoven, present a sea of sparkling green, plumed with fountains and surmounted by walls and trellis, or *accoudoirs*, of pleached limes. But, oddly enough, more colour and bolder pattern is provided by the *potager*, one of Dr Carvallo's happiest reconstructions, on the lower level of the garden by the moat. Here nine squares are surrounded by trellis, punctuated by rose-wreathed arbours: the squares are outlined in box and all in different shapes, but – and here is the stroke of genius – each bed contains a different variety of vegetable: and the contrasting foliages, blue-green cabbage, purple beet, jade-green carrot leaves and golden maize, present an opalescent chequerboard of colour on a scale which must surely be very rare.

Dr Carvallo thought that the English show too great a regard for Nature in planning their gardens, and wrote:

Nature, it is held, exists solely to subserve the needs and divine intelligence of mankind, or his subordinates the brutes, and is only tolerable on the human plane, as a garden, when remoulded in humanised forms or at least, in forms prescribed by the human intellect. 'Unnatural' as this wonderful formal garden is to English eyes, it is by that much the more 'human'. Indeed it is incomparably the most human garden in Europe in that, large as it is, the scale is perfectly adjusted to human capacities. There are no daunting baroque vistas; it is functionally appointed for human needs – the growing of vegetables, the enjoyment of flowers, promenading in sun or shade – and all within a framework of intellectual instead of emotional art. As such it constitutes the classic type of the European garden.

Arbours of trellis and roses
A shaded walk of tailored trees

Dr Carvallo, who was much aided in his great work by his brilliant and artistic American wife, born Miss Anne Coleman of Philadelphia, died in 1936. His son François Carvallo maintains the garden and has added a great apple orchard on the hillside to the south of the garden. Here 1,824 apple-trees have been planted in forty-six intercrossing lines, just as one sees them in Du Cerceau's engravings. This *Couronne fruitière Renaissance* dominates the whole property.

The garden at Villandry is of great importance to the student of the history of garden design as it exemplifies – and is unique in doing so – the plan of a great garden of the early seventeenth century, before the whole conception and aim of garden design was changed by Le Nôtre and his followers. At Villandry, the idea still holds good of the *Hortus Inclusus*, though immensely enlarged and elaborated. The gardens are still enclosed, making rectangles confined by hedges, terraces and trellis; the whole surrounding countryside is not drawn into the garden plan, as it later was to be, as at Vaux-le-Vicomte and Versailles.

Levens Hall WESTMORLAND

The best preserved topiary garden in Britain

Beyond a spreading plant of Choisya ternata, called after the Swiss botanist M. J. D. Choisy (1799–1859), lies the unique garden of Levens

THE GREAT HOUSE OF LEVENS, on the banks of the River Kent in Westmorland, has existed in one form or another for centuries. The earliest house, with its peel tower, was built by the Redeman family as a stronghold from which to repel Scottish raiders. In 1489 Levens was sold to Alan Bellingham, a man of ambition and some wealth, which he had acquired by marrying an heiress and by various deals in real estate. A loyal friend, though famous for his quick temper, his character is summed up in a rhyme alluding to his social and at the same time martial disposition,

Amicus, amico Alanus
Belliger belligero Bellinghamus

It was the belligerent Alan's great-grandson James who, in the last years of Elizabeth's reign, transformed Levens from a dank and frowning Plantagenet fortress into the spacious and hospitable Elizabethan country house we see today. Levens remained in the Bellingham family for two hundred years, till the reign of James II, when the Bellingham of the day, another Alan, an 'ingenious but unhappy young man', lost a fortune at cards and had to sell Levens to James Grahame, a devoted follower and adherent of the unfortunate Stuart King. After the revolution of 1688, Grahame was several times in danger of being imprisoned for his too outspoken loyalty to King James, and it was possibly

RIGHT: *Yew in every diversity of form*

this uncertainty which prevented him altering the Elizabethan character of his house, already somewhat out of date; for this we must be grateful. But it did not deter him from embarking on an elaborate programme of garden planning, and it was James Grahame who laid out the gardens at Levens, which are today acclaimed as the most perfect topiary gardens in England, and so it follows, in the world.

Topiary (the word derives from the Greek *topos*, 'a place', and so *topiarius* came to mean 'the man in charge of the place', hence gardener), which we have come to think of as a typically English gardening art, was known to the Romans, and there are descriptions by Pliny the Younger of borders of clipped box in his villa in Tuscany. The Romans, it is thought, passed on the art to their subject races in the East: clipped shrubs and bay trees were features of the gardens of Baghdad, and at the Generalife gardens in Spain, described elsewhere in this book, the Moors lined courtyards with low hedges of shorn box and myrtle. Topiary was a feature of Italian Renaissance gardens and of the great gardens in France, but nowhere was it used so spectacularly as it was in English gardens, and topiary as a garden embellishment seems as English as the rose. Ever since its introduction, however, it has caused controversy. Early in the sixteenth century, Bacon only showed a qualified enthusiasm for it: 'I, for my part,' he wrote, 'do not like images cut out in Juniper, or other garden stuff: they be for children. But little low hedges, round, like welts, with some pretty pyramids, I like well.'

A hundred years later Addison deplored the art of topiary in *The Spectator*: 'Our trees rise in cones, globes and pyramids. We see the mark of the scissors upon every plant and bush. I do not know whether I am singular in my opinion, but for my own part, I would rather look upon a tree in all its luxuriancy and diffusion of boughs and branches, than when it is thus cut and trimmed into a mathematical figure: and cannot but fancy that an orchard in flower looks infinitely more delightful than all the little labyrinths of the most finished parterre.' And Richard Steele ridiculed topiary in a famous passage, in which he offered for imaginary sale:

> Adam and Eve in yew; Adam a little shattered by the fall of the tree of knowledge in the great storm: Eve and the serpent very flourishing.
> St George in box; his arms scarce long enough, but will be in a condition to stick the dragon by next April.
> A green dragon of the same, with a tail of ground ivy for the present.
> An old maid of honour in wormwood.
> A quickset hog, shot up into a porcupine.
> A lavender pig, with sage growing in his belly.

The work of these sharp pens soon swayed the taste of garden-owners all over the country: topiary, overnight, went out of fashion; the work of sharp axes followed. Magnificent gardens everywhere were devastated to make way for the new Romantic style. Levens, fortunately, escaped.

'Monsieur Beaumont' who laid out the garden at Levens

The east façade of Levens Hall

LEFT: *Wisteria and iris with the bulky forms of clipped yew beyond*

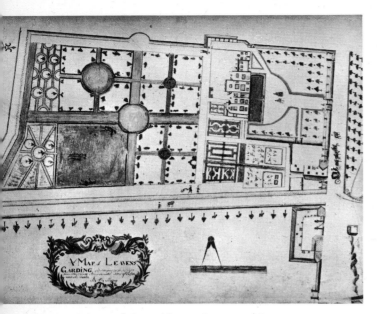

A map of the garden as it appeared in 1730

Beyond a spreading cedar, the tower of Levens Hall

The gardens at Levens were designed by a Frenchman, Beaumont, said to have been a pupil of Le Nôtre, though there is little in his plan for Levens, quite different in scale, size and feeling, to recall the work of Louis XIV's greatest of all gardeners; and the English gardens said to have been laid out to designs by Le Nôtre, who, in fact, never crossed the Channel, such as Bramham Park and Wrest, are entirely different. Beaumont, furthermore, is said to have had a hand in the design of the garden at Hampton Court, though his name does not figure in the *Warrants of Appointment* in the Ministry of Works' archives. But he certainly was responsible for Levens, where, on the staircase, his portrait hangs, 'Monsieur Beaumont, gardener to King James II and to Colonel J. Grahame. He laid out the gardens at Hampton Court and at Levens'. The gardener's house at Levens is, to this day, called Beaumont Hall.

The garden, though a unique example of its own curious style, is in no way grand. That great describer of gardens, the late H. Avray Tipping, has written: 'Indeed, that much misused word "quaint" is so appropriate that its use is excusable as describing the feeling that the Levens garden arouses.'

There is nothing of splendour of perspective, of grandeur of avenues sweeping towards the horizon at Levens, such as we see and admire in great continental gardens, or in some other English gardens of the period as drawn by Kniff and engraved by Kip. Rather do we find a great simplicity.

There is an extremely interesting map of the garden as it looked in 1730, forty years after its planting. This was made when Levens had passed into the possession of the Earl of Suffolk, who had married Catherine Grahame, Colonel Grahame's daughter and heiress. The map presents the whole picture. A carriage has just crossed the bridge over the Kent River and is drawing up at the gate in the balustrades which bounds the spacious courtyard. At the extreme end we see, and still see there today, the gateway to the stable yard with its high ball-capped piers. Nearby stands the gardener's house, 'Beaumont Hall'. The garden in the map displays a formal symmetry which, thanks to the passing years and the natural growth of the trees with which it is set, no longer exists. But it is the fantastic shapes which the yews and boxes at Levens have taken on which give the garden its special charm and mystery. Some of the original trees have disappeared, others have grown into one another; while here and there one has grown – the Great Umbrella for example – out of all proportion to its neighbours. Legend has named many of these trees, though it needs imagination to find any likeness between the group known as 'Queen Elizabeth and her Maids of Honour', described by a recent owner of Levens as representing the Queen and her ladies who 'would seem to have, close at hand, great jugs which, it must be presumed, are an allusion in topiary art to the strong beverage called "morocco" – a speciality of Levens'.

Morocco, a strong concoction with a base of beer and herbs and brewed in the Levens kitchen to a secret recipe, played an important part in the garden life at Levens, and was drunk, sometimes to excess, at the annual Radish Feast: this was held in the beech circle, a great circus of lawn enclosed in beech hedges, which, according to Mr Richard Bagot, 'have the advantage of keeping their russet-brown leaves throughout the long north country winter and spring, glowing red in the winter's sun – when the sun condescends to shine – or sparkling with hoar frost, and wrapped in a mantle of snow'.

Here the Mayor and Corporation of Kendal and the Westmorland neighbours feasted on brown bread and butter and radishes, of which vast quantities were brought to the scene of festivity in wheelbarrows. The feast ended in many toasts such as 'Luck to Levens while Kent flows' and general conviviality. A trace of these Radish Feasts was found half a century ago, when an ancient beer-mug was discovered in one of the hedges, completely grown into the wood: probably it had been thrown there by a reveller at the end of the feast, or in petulance when the supply of morocco ran out, though this was, it seems, a rare occurrence, for the conviviality of the Radish Feasts became something of a scandal, and they were finally discontinued.

But to return to the gardens: time and Nature have done much to obliterate the formal look which Monsieur Beaumont surely aimed at, and which certainly still existed, as we see from the plan, in 1730. In one part, however, south of the Broad Walk, which traverses the garden, lies an area of nearly five acres where, as the layout is on a larger scale, some formality of layout has survived. Here the imposing beech hedges, fifteen feet high and as much through, form allées and the splendid circus, and create an impression of ordered splendour of which Le Nôtre would thoroughly have approved.

In the nineteenth century Levens was lived in by a redoubtable woman, wife of a descendant of Lord Suffolk – Mrs Greville Howard, who reigned there for fifty years. While preserving the ancient character of the garden, and replacing 'in even lines the ductile yew', she made some additions of her own, thus slightly throwing out Monsieur Beaumont's plan. It was during Mrs Howard's time that the crowned lion, the Howard Crest, was added to the collection. Mrs Howard, a revered and matriarchal figure, died aged ninety-two in 1877. The present owner, Mr Robin Bagot, descends collaterally from her. He maintains the garden, and topiary needs a great deal of maintenance, exactly as she would have wished.

The garden at Levens is unique, and is worth any pains to preserve. It mercifully escaped the change of fashion which destroyed so many like it, and is in perfect harmony with the romantic old gabled house: its survival is a blessing, for there is no other topiary garden in the world to compare with this remarkable creation.

'It is the . . . shapes which the yews and boxes at Levens have taken on which give the garden its special charm and mystery'

The Vatican Garden ROME

The little-known garden behind St Peter's

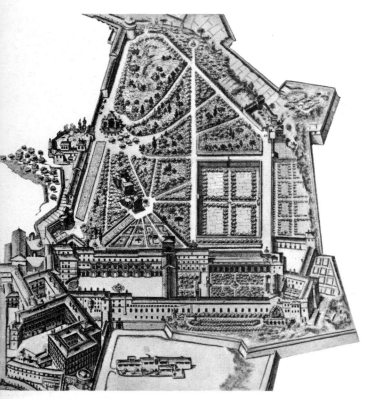

A print of the Vatican garden in 1670, showing the eagle fountain and the Villa Pia

SUMMER-HOUSES HAVE EVER BEEN delightful features of gardens the world over; but perhaps nowhere is there a summer-house of such pure enchantment as the Villa Pia in the gardens of the Vatican. The Villa Pia, built for the worldly and convivial Pope Pius IV in 1560 by the Neapolitan architect Pirro Ligorio, stands in the outer Vatican gardens, close by the Via Fondamenti. Behind it rises a steep hillside, the slopes of which were once clothed with cypresses, but have now given way to turf and scented shrubs. Ligorio, according to Percier and Fontaine, the architects of Napoleon, built the Villa Pia 'in the manner of the ancient houses, of which he had made a special study', and obviously it was inspired by the architecture and decoration of Pompeii and Herculaneum. But it is far from being a slavish imitation, the whole concept being instinct with Ligorio's own fantasy and taste.

The Villa Pia takes the form of an oval paved court with, on the north, an atrium, adorned with many-coloured mosaics, and on the south, an exquisitely proportioned pavilion, with an attic decorated with stucco plaques. At either end of the court are high, nobly architected gateways: these, again, are lavishly overlaid with stucco and mosaic. Encircling the courtyard is a low wall, with a marble bench all round, surmounted by graceful urns planted with aloes. In the centre is a fountain into which dolphins spew water, jockeyed by uproarious cupids. From this fountain the water flows underground to a tank on a lower level where sits Thetis, the Nereid mother of Achilles, on a watery throne, with a hassock of dripping leaves, ever freshened by the fountain's mist, at her feet.

The Villa Pia was described by Jacob Burckhardt, in his history of the Italian Renaissance as 'the most perfect retreat imaginable for a midsummer afternoon', and it is easy to see why it was the favourite place of resort of the cultured and gregarious Pius IV. The Holy Father, we are told, would pass whole days in his Casino in friendly discussion with the foremost intellectuals of the day, supping and sipping the hot afternoons away, and only returning to the Vatican in time for Vespers.

RIGHT: *A Roman matron, in marble, beneath a palm near the Pope's greenhouses*

Mosaic and the murmur of water in the Pope's retreat

Water plants, in mosaic, decorate a wall of Thetis' pool

The nereid Thetis on her watery throne at the Villa Pia, with St Peter's dome beyond

The architect, Pirro Ligorio, built this enchanting casino for Pope Pius IV in 1560

*The Villa Pia,
as it looked
two hundred
years ago*

61

'Angels' heads . . . continually appear as decorative motifs . . .'

An elaborate parterre of white gravel and cut turf

Much of the Vatican gardens has changed completely since the days of those pleasant symposia, although some features, such as the elaborate eagle-crowned fountain, have survived. But the gardens, as one sees them today, have the greatest charm, and make a cool oasis in the centre of the noise and hurry of modern Rome. The grass is fresh and green, the paths meticulously kept. Everywhere there are reminders that this is the garden of the Pope: angels' heads and the Tiara continually appear as decorative motifs, either carved in stone or clipped in box. But the ground the garden occupies once lay in the heart of pagan Rome, and pagan busts and classic sarcophagi meet one, too, at every turn. In the shady *Bosco* fragments of heathen sculpture have been built into garden seats, to aid a Cardinal's meditations or lull the siesta of a Legate.

One characteristic of the Vatican garden is unusual – the plants themselves. In too many Italian gardens flowers and rare plants are completely absent, and it is possible that in most they would seem redundant. Who looks for bright colours at Tivoli, for instance, or for botanic rarities in the Boboli? But in the Vatican Garden it is different: here the eye of the horticulturally inclined visitor is constantly taken by interesting plants. One border roofed with glass, for instance, houses a fine collection of succulents and tender plants, while elsewhere in the garden a wall of rusticated stone, in the true tradition of the classic Italian garden, instead of being abandoned to the usual maiden-hair and moss, has been planted (dare one mention the word when describing a garden in Rome?) as an extremely effective rock-garden.

RIGHT: *A giant pine grows by Pope Pius' casino*

Bomarzo NEAR VITERBO

A giant-haunted grove in the Cimini Hills

Giants in mortal combat

MYSTERY ENSHROUDS THE HISTORY OF the garden made by Pier Francesco Orsini, at Bomarzo. Descriptions of it make one wonder if such a place can really exist – a garden, or was it a garden? – set, not with trees, flowers and fountains, but peopled with monstrous statues, carved from the living rock, each stranger and more fantastic than the last. Were they the work, as village legend holds, of Turkish prisoners-of-war captured at Lepanto? Or were they, as more informed research would have them, inspired by the imagination and fantasy of Orsini himself, a Renaissance dilettante, who may have been bored by the rigid convention and fashion in contemporary garden design. For there is little plan about the way the statues are arranged – no overall scheme seems to link them.

Whatever their history, the *Mostre di Bomarzo* do exist. The astonished visitor will find gigantic statues, of a mermaid, half woman, half sea-serpent, a dragon, a lion, and one of Hannibal's elephants complete with castle, in the act of mangling a Roman soldier. One female figure bears a vase of iris on her head, some of the few flowers to be seen at Bomarzo; while nearby, cut into the hillside, a giant gapes and offers the hospitality of his mouth to picnickers, or lovers.

For centuries this garden has been called the *Sacro Bosco*, but there is little sacred about Bomarzo – rather the opposite, in spite of its guardian chapel surrounded by stones carved with symbols of death. The sacred wood and its denizens was little known outside the immediate neighbourhood for many years. Augustus Hare, in his *Walks Near Rome*, published in the eighties of the last century, although he visited Bomarzo, does not mention the monsters. But recently they have been re-discovered, and yearly attract many visitors. Perhaps the originality and humour of Pier Francesco Orsini's conception have more appeal today than they had before; for as we visit the great Renaissance gardens of Italy, their symmetry, their ordered line, their very perfection can pall and their urbanities satiate. After them Bomarzo comes as a shock, an exclamation mark. It offers the thrill of the unexpected and, perhaps even more, of the unexplained.

RIGHT: *The inscription on the giant's upper lip reads 'ogni pensiero voi'. Its mouth offers hospitality to 'any philosophers'*

Giants in stone in an Italian landscape

'One of Hannibal's elephants . . . mangling a Roman soldier'

On a smiling hill-side near Viterbo, the astonished visitor will find them

ABOVE: *A face framed in foliage*

LEFT: *A vast mermaid bears a vase of verdure*

EXTREME LEFT: *The chapel, guardian of the so-called* Sacro Bosco

67

Vaux-le-Vicomte SEINE-ET-MARNE

The first masterpiece of André le Nôtre

André Le Nôtre (1613–1700) the greatest of all garden architects

ON A WARM AUGUST EVENING IN 1661 the newly finished château and gardens of Vaux-le-Vicomte presented a scene of splendour such as France had seldom seen before, and Vaux-le-Vicomte was never to see again. Nicolas Fouquet, *Surintendant des Finances de France*, was entertaining the youthful King Louis XIV. The King was accompanied by the Queen Mother, the zestful, pregnant, but quite undeterred Duchesse d'Orléans, Henriette d'Angleterre, and an immense train of courtiers.

The reception was on a gigantic scale and lasted nearly twelve hours, beginning in the afternoon and continuing, punctuated by collations and suppers, until the small hours of the following morning. The daunting programme included a comedy, written by Molière in less than a fortnight especially for the occasion – his *Facheux de Vaux*, acted in a *théâtre de verdure* designed by Giacomo Torelli in the garden. The play was followed by a ballet to the accompaniment of music by Lully played by orchestras of twenty-four violins hidden in the surrounding bosquets. The entertainment was opened by a leading Paris actress, Madeleine Béjart, emerging from a shell and singing an ode to the King, *Aussi doux que sévère, aussi puissant que juste*. It ended with the appearance in the canal of a whale belching fire and smoke, which was the signal for a firework display which seemed to roof the whole garden with light, and was so deafening that the Queen Mother's carriage-horses bolted, and the guests were reminded of the cannonades of the Fronde. All through the exhausting programme the King seemed delighted. But the very magnificence of the entertainment may have confirmed the doubts as to Fouquet's honesty. The grandeur of Vaux was so overpowering that its gardens made those at Versailles, then hardly started, seem like the pleasure grounds of a mere *gentil-hommière*. Some say that the King had already determined to arrest Fouquet; others, that he was still in doubt, and that the ostentation at Vaux tipped the scales. After all, the room in which the King ate one of his three suppers had a ceiling upon which Le Brun had painted 'The Triumph of Truth', and supper was served off gold plate: there was no gold plate at Versailles.

RIGHT: *High over the water of the* théâtre d'eau *prance web-footed horses*

VAUX-LE-VICOMTE

Harmony achieved by clipped yews, noble statuary and regimented trees

The grand entrance to the château is screened by a high grille with piers of weathered stone

By the time the fête ended, as dawn of the next day broke, the King appeared silent and thoughtful; but everyone agreed that his farewell to his host was particularly charming and condescending: 'I cannot ask you to visit me at Versailles,' he said. 'You would be inconvenienced.' Irony? Perhaps, because a fortnight later Fouquet was arrested for peculation and imprisoned. It is said that he had half hoped that, at his great party, the King would have offered him the highest position in France, that of First Minister, who held the seals of France. 'He has his seals now', said the Chancellor Séguier grimly, as he fixed them on the doors and cabinets of Fouquet's great property, following its sequestration.

Nicolas Fouquet, young, brilliant, unscrupulous and a connoisseur, adored making money – and love. (One theory of his downfall was that he had cast his eye on the King's mistress, Mlle de la Vallière.) He was thirty-six at the time of the famous fête. Generous in his patronage of artists such as Le Brun, Le Sueur and writers like Molière, the vast fortune he had gained while in office had raised Mazarin's suspicions. The young Colbert had been placed in his office with orders from the Cardinal to find out what he could. The Cardinal died before any tangible proof was found, but not before he had breathed his suspicions to the already jealous King: hence the arrest, and Fouquet's imprisonment and death nineteen years later. His motto was *Quo non ascendam*. His device was a squirrel, a squirrel leaping upward from branch to branch – 'What height can I

Le Nôtre believed that the main layout of a garden should at once be apparent. The south parterre

not attain?' The squirrel appears in many forms at Vaux, painted on ceilings or carved in stone. An eighteenth-century visitor has described a sculptured lion in the garden, curiously naïve in the circumstances, bearing the cognisance of Fouquet, and a cornucopia, with a squirrel nibbling the falling fruit. Poor Fouquet – in his portrait which still hangs at Vaux he looks rather like a squirrel himself, bright-eyed and sharp-nosed, and his nibbling was on so vast a scale that from living in the most splendid private house in France he died in a prison cell. But he left, in the Château of Vaux-le-Vicomte and its gardens, an unparalleled legacy to France.

The château, planned on a scale unheard of at the time, was begun in the year 1656. It is approached through an imposing *cour d'entrée* enclosed in a wrought-iron railing of great delicacy, with pillars, which are its chief beauty, modelled by Poissant and sculpted with the heads of gods and goddesses. The celebrated gardens are first seen from the terrace to the south of the château. Wide and far they lie, like a gigantic Aubusson. They were designed by Le Nôtre, 'the gardener of Kings, and King of gardeners'.

André Le Nôtre's father had been Marie de Medici's gardener at the Tuileries, and he first apprenticed his son to Simon Vouet, painter to the King. Here the young Le Nôtre was brought into early contact with artists like Le Sueur, Mignard and Le Brun: these may well have influenced his eye and helped him to conceive the vast and gracious perspectives which he would one day

A distant view of Fouquet's château from the immense garden

The supreme example of French garden design

A beast of stone, half-hound, half-lion, and a graventerm by the edge of a glade

The Great Canal, where at Fouquet's fête, a whale appeared, belching fire. Beyond lies the grotto

How the garden at Vaux-le-Vicomte looked in the seventeenth century

The great parterre with its elaborat

The seven alcoved grotto of rusticate

*broderies of meticulously clipped box and rosy powdered brick
stone: water gods recline at either end*

73

conjure, not in paint, but in the living, growing landscape.

Le Nôtre soon, however, reverted to his father's trade and studied practical gardening in the gardens of the Tuileries, though the tasks allotted him do not seem to have been very responsible ones; the care of a trellis of jasmine and of some bushes of white mulberries were two of them. When he was forty, his first important assignment came, when Fouquet, then at the height of his power, heard of him from Le Brun and asked him to design the gardens at Vaux: here the works when completed were reputed to have cost eighteen million francs, a fantastic sum; of this a high proportion was spent on the garden.

The perceptive visitor, standing on the terrace of the château, will see at once that the site presented difficulties: the ground slopes from west to east. This fact Le Nôtre disguised with a plantation of trees on one side and a raised terrace on the other. Between lies a vast parterre embellished by statues and fountains, and intersected by gravelled paths into smaller parterres of *broderies* outlined in clipped box and filled with pink *brique pilée* (crushed brick). These the present owner of the château, Madame Sommier and her late husband, have restored exactly to the state in which they were in Fouquet's day.

The parterre is traversed by a wide canal, invisible, owing to the fall in the ground, from the terrace, and beyond that again lies a larger canal, also invisible from the terrace, separated from the parterre by a high colonnade of rusticated stone. This is the most striking feature of the garden, the famous *théâtre d'eau*, in which the whale, at Fouquet's great reception, made its single, sensational appearance.

This fall in levels, and the fact that the components of the garden reveal themselves only gradually as one draws further away from the château, makes a visit to the gardens at Vaux a series of delightful adventures.

The balustrade surmounting the colonnade is laced with fountains, while twin flights of steps lead down to the lower level, where it becomes apparent that the high terrace is supported by seven graceful arches in the form of grottoes, and that on each side there are stalactite-hung caves, in which are reclining statues impersonating rivers, each with a symbolic, gushing urn. Looking away from these across the second canal, the eye is led by a broad tree-lined vista to a heroic statue on the skyline, of the Farnese Hercules, almost as large as the one at Wilhelmshöhe at Kassel.

After the fall of Fouquet all his protégés, though most were grateful to their first patron, naturally turned their faces towards the Sun King, then just embarking on his development of Versailles. These were the gardens which were to immortalize the name of Le Nôtre, and make it a household-word for all gardeners. It is ironical to think that, but for Vaux-le-Vicomte, his greatest extravagance, the name of Fouquet, the squirrel who nibbled too much, would be almost forgotten.

Ganymede, cupbearer to the Gods

A trio of cherubs hold aloft a basket of fruit

LEFT: *A statue of Autumn by Girardon – bare-footed, with sheaves of corn*

Williamsburg VIRGINIA

A masterly reconstruction of the 18th century

A CHANCE CONVERSATION BETWEEN a clergyman and a businessman at an official luncheon might not ordinarily be expected to
lead to sensational results, but when the businessman was John
D. Rockefeller, Jr, one of the richest men in the world, and the
clergyman the Reverend Dr William A. R. Goodwin, the result
was different: for the clergyman had a dream which was almost
an obsession: the dream of seeing his beloved Williamsburg,
where he was rector of Bruton Parish Church, restored to its
eighteenth-century beauty.

In 1699 Williamsburg succeeded Jamestown as the capital of
the English colony of Virginia, of which for eighty years it was
not only the centre of Government, but also the social and cultural hub. Elected Burgesses, too, treated their families to a
taste of city life when they came to Williamsburg to deliberate
on the affairs of the Colony. Here the wealthy tobacco planters
brought their families to town several times a year, to breathe
the air of polite society. They found the business and social
round a full one, with court sessions and tobacco sales in the day-
time, and balls and routs at night: the streets were filled with
smart equipages and lined with elegant shops: there were excellent inns, the Raleigh Tavern among them. But the planters'
ladies soon wanted their own establishments in the gay capital,
and building started apace. Delightful medium-sized houses, of
rosy brick, or crisp weatherboard, sprang up everywhere. Centre
of social life was the Governor's Palace, a high cupola'd building
with airy wrought-iron gates and gate-piers surmounted by the
Lion and Unicorn of England. Nightly these gates swung open
to let in a throng of guests. The palace was set in a splendid garden, and all about, round the smaller houses of Williamsburg,
were other gardens, formal and neat with clipped box-hedges
and bricked paths. Not for the citizens of Williamsburg were the
wild, natural gardens then coming into fashion in England; the
real wild was quite near enough in eighteenth-century Virginia,
and at home they wanted to forget it and create around their
houses a little ordered world of formality which reminded them
of their grandparents' gardens in England.

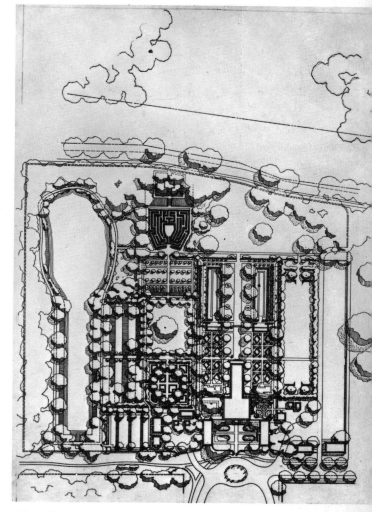

*Plan of the Governor's Palace garden at Williamsburg,
as it is today*

LEFT: *A geometric pattern of gravel paths, mown grass and clipped box hedging*

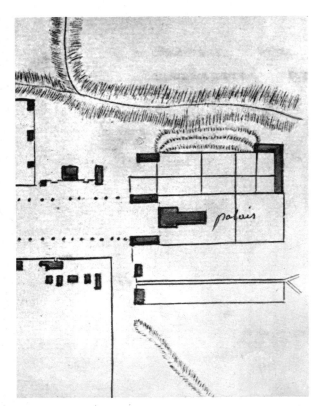

The Governor's Palace as indicated on 'the French-man's map'; one of the earliest maps of Williamsburg

A seat of white painted Chinoiserie, in an all-green setting of clipped box, mown grass and beds close set with periwinkle

This period of Williamsburg's history lasted for about eighty years. Then, in 1781, when the capital of Virginia was moved to Richmond, the fortunes and importance of Williamsburg began to fall. People moved away from the city, and the Governor's Palace was destroyed by fire, as was the Capitol building some years later. In the nineteenth century the decay went on. Beautiful Georgian buildings were altered beyond recognition or pulled down to make way for hotels, offices and shops. But something remained: among the eighty Colonial structures surviving the passage of time were a number of brick and frame houses, the Bruton Parish Church, which had been built in 1715, and The College of William and Mary (the oldest College after Harvard in all America) of which the central block was said to have been designed by Sir Christopher Wren.

Amid the spoliation and vulgarization there was enough left to set Dr Goodwin dreaming of a Williamsburg restored, which would leave to the American people a constant reminder of how a state capital looked in Colonial days. Late in the 'twenties, the momentous meeting with J. D. Rockefeller took place. Such was Goodwin's eloquence and enthusiasm that he was able to fire Rockefeller's imagination too. Millions of dollars were made available for the restoration, and in 1927 work began. Williamsburg became the scene of intense activity, which entailed the restoration and reconstruction of much of the most important parts of the town to the appearance they had in Colonial days. Since the work began, more than eighty colonial buildings have been restored. More than half the major buildings along mile-long Duke of Gloucester Street and its immediate neighbourhood are original, while scores of others have been rebuilt on their original foundations to complete the scene.

Certain firm rules governed the restoration: one was that 'within the restoration area all work which no longer represents Colonial or classical traditions should be demolished or removed': and another stipulates that 'no surviving old work should be rebuilt for structural reasons if any reasonable additional trouble and expense would suffice to preserve it'. Above all, when it was absolutely necessary to use new building material, such as bricks, stones, tiles and so on, 'no attempt should be made to "antique" them by theatrical means'.

The result of this conscientious, honest and loving labour is transcendantly successful. Today the main street of the town, called after the eighteenth-century Duke of Gloucester, lined with debonair Georgian houses, some imposing, some quite modest, presents the verdant appearance, with its hedges, tree-lined squares and many gardens, of an eighteenth-century street.

Gardens, too, play an important part in creating the illusion of Williamsburg: and the re-creation there of period gardens, large and small, has been particularly happy. Great care has been taken to trace, from the foundations of the old walls and partitions, their original design. In the garden of the Governor's

Palace and other Williamsburg gardens, only plants have been used which could have grown there in Colonial days, so the visitor will look in vain, for instance, for polyantha roses, as these were unknown in the eighteenth century. Joan Parry Dutton in her book *Enjoying America's Gardens* has written: 'The reconstructed garden of the Governor's Palace at Williamsburg is one of the very few remaining examples of the perfect eighteenth-century garden; in fact its only counterpart is the reconstructed garden at Villandry in Touraine, France.' Other eighteenth-century gardens have been altered, new styles and new plant material added, but in the Palace garden, everything is as closely authentic as existing evidence allows.

The garden of the Palace is most imposing, and in it are to be found many of the features of the eighteenth century: classic box-bordered parterres, a canal, a bowling green, warm walls of brick for growing fruit and espaliered apple and pear trees. But there are two features which few would think of including when planning a modern garden. The first is a Mount, a raised hillock built over the underground ice house from which the whole garden can be surveyed, a survival from mediaeval times and an amenity warmly praised by Bacon is his famous essay on gardens: 'I wish also, in the very middle, a fair mound with three ascents . . . ' But mounts were known in America centuries before they were known in Europe, for the prehistoric inhabitants of the Mississippi and Ohio Valleys reared them, for some mysterious religious reason, in many forms, circular or pointed, or even in the form of animals. The other outstanding feature of the garden of the Governor's Palace is the Maze, said to be modelled on the one at Hampton Court using the native American holly as the basic plant material.

All around the Governor's Palace lie the other, smaller properties of Williamsburg, each, in its individual way, combining the units that were considered essential for a property two hundred years ago: a small pleasure ground, a potager, stables, paddocks, smoke-houses, out-buildings, privies and orchards. The general impression of these smaller gardens is one of neat compactness; almost all are set in a framework of green, and the green is usually provided by box-hedges, not always clipped, but often left to grow unrestricted, sometimes into trees thirty feet high: in fact, the tangy scent of box on a hot afternoon is something that visitors to Williamsburg always remember. Other shades of green are offered by plantings of ground-cover, like English ivy and the box-edged beds of periwinkle in the garden of the Governor's Palace, and the typical American use of permanent plantings, economical and goodlooking even in winter, of yew, holly, magnolias, pine, cedar and other conifers.

Though the gardens of Colonial Williamsburg are conscientiously planted only with trees, flowers and shrubs known to have been grown there in the eighteenth century, the variety of the plant material is still surprisingly great. Many of the finest

A narrow path, gravelled and dappled with sunshine, under a canopy of pleached lime-trees

79

The Royal Lion and Unicorn of England still guard
the main entrance of the Palace

Diamond-shaped beds of clipped box and periwinkle

The eighteenth century lives again

Fruit trees espaliered as they were in the time of William and Mary

The garden seen through the East Gate, a masterly recreation of early eighteenth-century ironwork

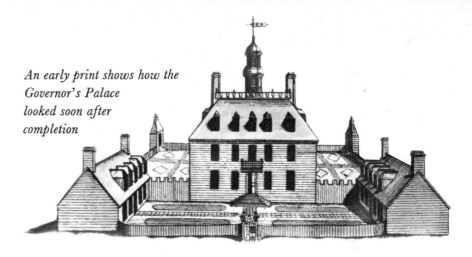

An early print shows how the Governor's Palace looked soon after completion

trees are American natives, and from America they have been sent all over the world: trees such as the American Linden, *Tilia americana*, and the Hornbeam, *Carpinus carolinianum*, and *Nyssa sylvatica*, which burns so bright in autumn, and its flaming rival, the scarlet oak, *Quercus coccinea*.

Box, as we have seen, though originally imported from England, was a stand-by in Colonial gardens, but there were other useful endemic evergreens as well, such as the Yaupon holly, *Ilex vomitoria*, which lends itself well to clipping, and the American Holly, *Ilex opaca*; and every writer on Virginia gardens extolls the most beautiful of all American natives, the wonderful *Magnolia grandiflora*, which lays its fragrance on the air at Williamsburg at every turn during the summer months.

The student of gardening can learn many lessons from the gardens of Williamsburg. He can learn how his garden can be given a clothed and luxuriant look even in the depths of winter by generous plantings of evergreens of contrasting foliage, and he can learn how in the smallest garden, simplicity can create an air of pleasing formality, which is much enhanced by a high standard of detail in workmanship; the perfectly proportioned path, for instance, or well chosen brickwork or the delicate design of a picket fence.

The motto of Colonial Williamsburg, 'That the future may learn from the past', is apt indeed.

OPPOSITE:

TOP: *The ballroom wing of the Governor's Palace from the north-west*

BOTTOM: *Gates of airy wrought-iron between sturdy piers of brick*

Tulips and other spring flowers fill box-bordered beds in the Palace garden

Versailles

The greatest garden in the world

On the Parterre d'Eau. La Seine by Le Hongre

LOUIS XIV, THE CREATOR OF VERSAILLES, himself wrote in 1689 a guide for visitors to his famous palace and gardens. His words. are instinct, not only with pride in his fabulous domain, but also with a host's kindliness and hope that his guests should enjoy their visit, and see the palace and gardens at their best. In his *Manner of seeing the gardens at Versailles* he writes: 'On quitting the Château by the Entrance Hall of the *Cour de Marbre*, we gain the grounds. We must stop at the top of the steps to consider the disposition of the parterres, the ornamental waters and fountains in the arbours.' The Sun King continues: 'Then we must go straight to the terrace above the fountain of Latona, and pause to consider here, the lizards, the steps, the statues, the royal avenue, Apollo, the canal, and then turn to look back at the parterre and the Château.'

The visitor to Versailles today would do well to follow the King's instructions. After passing through the Palace and entering the gardens, this is the panorama which spreads before him, exactly as it did three hundred years ago. Ahead, the *Parterre d'Eau*, twin rectangles of water which shimmeringly reflect the long low façade of the Château. To right and left, the parterres of lawn and flowers and broderies of low clipped box. Further to the left lies the Orangerie, under the *Ailes des Princes*. Further to the right, but hidden by trees, lies the *Bassin du Dragon*. Following His Majesty's advice, the visitor walks away from the Château, between the two *pièces d'eau*, towards the terrace above the fountain of Latona. Here an extension to the panorama greets his eye. Beyond the fountain lie the twin lower parterres, and in the centre and beyond, the famous *tapis vert*, stretching between high trees interspersed with urns and statues to the *Bassin d'Apollon* and the Great Canal. This is over a mile long, although, owing to foreshortening, it appears much less.

Louis XIII, father of Louis XIV, at the age of six enjoyed his first hunt in the woods round the village of Versailles. The bag was a leveret, some quails and two partridges: not bad for a child of six. Twenty years later, as King, married, but dreadfully bored by his wife and the intrigues of Court life in Paris, he re-

RIGHT: *The fountain of Latona and the Tapis Vert beyond*

turned more and more to Versailles, sleeping in the inn, or even, according to Saint-Simon, camping in the windmill. Delighted with the quiet and solitude of the place, he soon built a small château as a hunting lodge. There exists no record of the gardens, but it is likely that they were laid out by Jacques Boyceau, Controller-general of the gardens of the Royal Residences. Soon the King gave orders for trees to be planted, and the long story of the gardens and park of Versailles began.

Gradually more land was acquired. Parterres were designed by Jacques de Menours, Boyceau's nephew, and more water was led to the Park from the lake at Clagny. The *Rondeau des Cygnes*, a circular lake for swans, was dug, which eventually was enlarged into the *Bassin d'Apollon*. To match the growing grandeur of the garden (the garden at Versailles always seemed to exceed the Palace in importance, which had to grow to keep pace with it), the Château itself was enlarged and elaborated in 1613 by Philibert Le Roy. An engraving exists of this new building, by Israil Sylvestre, and depicts the side facing the gardens.

In 1643 Louis XIII died and was succeeded by a child of four – Louis XIV. Versailles was deserted, and although the new King occasionally visited it for hunting, it fell into some neglect. But Louis must have retained an affection for the place, with its memories of his father, for in 1660, the year before the dramatic fête at Vaux, he, too, started to develop Versailles. Two neighbouring villages were acquired – Trianon, whose name has survived, and Choisy-aux-Boeufs, which has not. Most important of all, he had André Le Nôtre to help him. The fame of Le Nôtre, whose career we have traced in our description of Vaux, rests on his work at Versailles. With a brilliant elasticity of mind, he tailored his designs to the topography of the ground. When this was absolutely impossible, the arrangement was reversed and the topography altered to suit the design.

Versailles is the perfect example of Le Nôtre's art. The landscape has been completely subjugated to the taste of the seventeenth century: trees are tonsured, and pieces of water laid to lighten the cold perfection of the perspective with their glimpses of the sky, where we are almost surprised to see the still untutored clouds sail by. Statues of gods and goddesses themselves stand meekly by, like lackeys, in stony servitude; deities no more, degraded by the architects of the King of France.

The site could hardly have been worse for a Palace and garden on the scale that the King obviously envisaged. Saint-Simon called it the saddest and most barren of all places, 'with no view, no water, no wood – for it is all shifting sand and marsh'; and Colbert, the enemy of Fouquet, who controlled the King's purse-strings and feared more extravagance on the scale of Vaux-le-Vicomte, implored the King not to embark on a grandiose project in such an unpromising position. The King was undeterred: '*C'est dans les choses difficiles*,' he wrote complacently, '*que nous faisons paraître notre vertu*'.

' Louis the Sun King, young and ardent . . .' Detail of a vase carved by Le Goulon

A marble vase by the Tapis Vert

LEFT: *La Saone, 'a luscious woman, attended by a laughing cupid' with some grapes*

Statues by the Bassin d'Apollon

So the work on the gardens and park proceeded, and was not to stop for fifty years. Every day four hundred labourers were employed moving earth. The great artificial plateau, with its parterres of flowers and water in front of the Château, was laboriously constructed. The menagerie, usually housing a rather dull collection of animals – one cage contained sheep – was constructed, and has now completely disappeared. At either end of the *Tapis Vert* there were changes, and in 1670 the fountain of Latona was constructed and Louis XIII's simple *Rondeau des Cygnes* was enlarged and became the *Bassin d'Apollon*. In 1672 the *Parterre d'Eau* was laid out. The Orangerie, as it exists today, was finished in 1683, in which year the stretch of water known as the *Pièce des Suisses*, because a regiment of Swiss soldiers had been employed in digging it, was first filled. By this time the garden of Versailles had taken on the form and plan that we see today, and had become the wonder and envy of the civilized world. One of the reasons why Louis XIV and his Court made such an overwhelming imprint on, and impressed so deeply, a wondering Europe, was that they had created their own world, and were totally, and irritatingly self-sufficient. Whatever the King of England and the King of Spain might devise, the King of France had done, in fact, better, and on a vaster scale: architecture, literature, conversation, landscape gardening, cooking,

even hunting. In fact, any of the pursuits which elevate or divert the spirits of man, were seen at Versailles at their best, and were practised there to greater perfection than anywhere else. So the world tried, usually but indifferently, to copy, and the French way of life became the pattern for Europe.

In 1715 Louis XIV, the Merlin who had conjured the marvel of Versailles, died. Under the Regency, the Palace and garden were for some years neglected, although they were still one of the sights that visitors had to see. Among them was Peter the Great, who examined the fountains with an engineer's expert eye and induced the architect Le Blond to follow him to Russia, where he employed him in the design for Peterhof and its magnificent fountains.

In 1722 the Court returned to Versailles, to the plaudits and acclamation of the people of the town, which had suffered poverty during its absence. Louis XV, who never liked the lack of privacy entailed by his great-grandfather's public way of life, altered the interior of the Château radically to create the famous *petits appartements*, in which the monarch could be alone with a few chosen favourites. He wanted, too, to make the gardens less formal, but lack of funds prevented him. In his reign, the changes to the gardens were few, although a passing interest in botany, or more likely a sudden passion for strawberries, led

VERSAILLES

The two syllables of Versailles evoke la grande époque

The children on the sphinxes in marble and bronze by Jacques Sarrazin have been a joy to the gardens since 1660

The Tapis Vert, with Aria and Poetus by Coysevox

Marble vases line the Tapis Vert

The ships on the Grand Canal were rigged in gold and silver

'Statues of gods and goddesses ... stand meekly by ... in stony servitude'

91

Artemis on the North Parterre

The colonnade, of which Mansard was the architect

him to establish at Trianon a botanical garden under Claude Richard, described by Linnaeus as being the ablest gardener of the age, and Bernard de Jussieu, known as the Newton of botany. So much time did the King spend in this new garden that a small house had to be constructed for his convenience and the Petit Trianon was the result. The east façade of this exquisite building, designed by Louis himself, Madame de Pompadour and the architect Gabriel between them, looked over the new botanical garden, with its hothouses and beds of rare plants. Flowers and fruit, and strawberries, especially in the dining-room, were much used in the decoration of the enchanting interior.

In 1774 Louis XV was succeeded by his grandson, Louis XVI, and it was about this time that the gardens of Versailles were denuded of their trees, many of the full-grown limes planted by Le Nôtre in the early days having never entirely recovered from being transplanted so late in life. Early in the new reign it was decided to cut most of these down and replant the allées and bosquets afresh, and with a more varied assortment of trees, chosen with more regard for the exigencies of the soil. Thus many lime trees and chestnuts were replaced by maples, planes and cedars. After the wholesale felling the gardens presented a forlorn spectacle, as we can see from Hubert Robert's picture.

Louis XVI gave the Petit Trianon to Marie Antoinette, who finding little to alter inside, at once set about changing the garden. *Le style anglais* had become fashionable, and Le Nôtre's noble perspectives seemed out of date. Most of Richard's botanic garden was swept away, and the Comte de Caraman, whose garden in the English-Chinese style had been admired by the Queen, was appointed Director of her gardens. Money was poured away (for simplicity is often expensive) creating a new natural landscape, with a mountain, groves, a grotto and a small lake overlooked by a charming belvedere designed by Mique, who also designed the nearby Temple of Love, which shelters a sculpture by Bouchardon of Cupid making himself a bow from Hercules' club. All these alterations gave rise to rumours of the Queen's extravagance and foreshadowed her unpopularity; but so delightful did she find the intimacy and peace of Trianon, that in 1783 she had constructed, again to the design of Mique, the famous *Hameau* where she and her intimate friends played an elaborate, and in retrospect, touching, game of 'Let's pretend'. By now the great days of Versailles were nearly over, and *le déluge* foreseen by Louis XV was about to break. The news of the Revolution reached the Queen at Trianon while she was sitting in the garden, pensive and sad, for recently she had lost her eldest son. The next day, 5th October 1789, the agony of the French monarchy began, when the Royal Family left for Paris – never to return. As he stepped into his coach, the King said sadly to the director of the Palace: 'You are now master here; try to save my poor Versailles'.

Felling the trees at Versailles in 1774–5, by Hubert Robert

Although the Château was stripped of its furniture, the gardens of Versailles suffered, as it happened, comparatively little in the Revolution, though at one point a plan was drawn up for their partition. But they were, of necessity, neglected; grass grew on the terraces and the Grand Canal was choked with reeds. To save the parterres, and prove their usefulness, the gardeners planted them with potatoes.

Napoleon did not care for Versailles, but he gave orders that the park should once more be put in order. The gardens had a narrow escape under the Empire; at one point it was suggested that all the statues, now completely demodé, should be scrapped and replaced with 'panoramas of masonry', representing famous towns captured by the *Grande Armée*. Mercifully, this scheme was never put into effect, and the gardens remained largely unchanged. Both the Trianons played a part under the Empire. The ravishing Princess Pauline lived at Le Petit Trianon, and Madame Mère at Le Grand. Almost the last meeting between Napoleon and Joséphine took place at Le Grand Trianon, at a disastrous luncheon at which no one spoke a word.

The Restoration affected Versailles but little. The gardens were maintained, but neither Louis XVIII nor Charles X ever lived in the Château itself, the future of which had now become

Bernard de Jussieu, known as the Newton of Botany

VERSAILLES

Statues against a tapestry of leaves

something of a problem. It was the mediocre King Louis Philippe who acquired the throne, somewhat dubiously, in 1830, who must receive credit for the final preservation of Versailles. The Château was turned into a museum dedicated to all the glories of France, and the Château and gardens recognized as one of the country's most precious national possessions. Its future was, and still is, assured.

Returning to the part of the garden from which Louis XIV himself suggested Versailles should be viewed, the terrace above the fountain of Latona, we can examine some of the treasures of sculpture with which the gardens are embellished. Facing the façade of the Château, we have on either side the twin rectangles of water of the *parterre d'eau*. Around these are bronzes of an incomparable beauty. At the corners of each bassin are statues by Tubi, Le Hongre, Coysevox and Regnaudin, of reclining figures representing the rivers of France, the most charming perhaps, being the Saone by the Italian Tubi – a luscious woman, attended by a laughing cupid.

It must be remembered that when originally placed in position and up to the Revolution, much of the lead sculpture at Versailles was gilded, which gave the gardens, with its many coloured flowers blooming under halcyon skies, an indescribable brilliance.

How immeasurably much remains. The word Versailles is like a cry across the years. In it there seems to be something of a call to arms, or the note of a violin, or the scream of a rocket mounting. In two syllables it evokes the *grande époque* and the half-century that followed. But as we read it, we think, out of all that silken throng, of two people only – Marie Antoinette, certainly, the Queen of whom Edmund Burke wrote his famous lines, 'Surely never lighted on this orb, which she hardly seemed to touch, a more delightful vision . . . glittering like the morning star, full of life, and splendour and joy.' But first and foremost, Louis XIV himself – Louis the Sun King, young and ardent, Louis *le Grand Monarque* with his receding brow and towering wig. For Louis is Versailles, and Versailles, Louis.

View of Versailles in 1682

RIGHT : *Endless flower-filled vistas of the garden at Versailles*

Peterhof LENINGRAD

Peter the Great's Versailles by the sea

'Something magnificent in all this gold, outdoors, in a country with the rudest climate in Europe ...'

ON THE DEATH OF LOUIS XIV in 1715, and the ending of much of the work at Versailles, many of the architects and designers who had been in the employ of the Sun King had to look for fresh fields for their activities. Some went to Russia, lured there by the lavish promises of Peter the Great. Peter, a big man with big ideas, wanted one of Louis XIV's own architects to take over the planning of his new capital of St Petersburg, and to build near it a Russian equivalent of Versailles. Leading the party of distinguished French artists, designers and sculptors to forsake France for Russia – then considered to be on the very fringe of civilization – was Alexandre Jean-Baptiste Le Blond.

Le Blond, from whose edition of d'Argenville's *La Théorie et la Pratique du Jardinage* we quote in our chapter on Schwetzingen, was a man of parts. He was an artist, and had himself delightfully illustrated his new edition of *La Théorie*; he had worked with the famous Le Nôtre at Versailles and elsewhere, and had been the architect of more than one distinguished building in Paris, the Hotel de Vendôme in the rue de l'Enfer among them. But garden design was his special study, 'having read a great many Latin, French and Spanish authors on the subject', and he referred to 'the abode I made at Paris and Versailles, whose neighbouring parts contain so many wonders of this nature, and the pains I have taken in planting several fine gardens'.

Le Blond was taken to meet Peter, who was then in Germany. They got on well and the young Frenchman – he was in his early thirties – was offered the splendid-sounding title of Architect-General of St Petersburg, at a salary, guaranteed for at least five years, of 5,000 roubles.

Peter wrote a warm recommendation of his new acquisition to his great friend and boon companion, Prince Menshikov in Russia. 'Welcome Le Blond ... and respect his contract ... he is an intelligent man and highly respected in the ateliers of France, so that, through him, we can engage whomsoever we will.' He went on to say that in future all the architects of St Petersburg should submit their plans to Le Blond for approval.

RIGHT: *The main cascade and water garden at Peterhof*

The Pavilion of Mon Plaisir built to the plans of Alexandre Le Blond

A canal runs below the palace terrace towards the sea

Le Blond, and a considerable party of colleagues and assistants, arrived in St Petersburg in the autumn of 1716. At once he set to work with his plans for further developing the new city, still less than fifteen years old. We need not examine his work there in detail; suffice it to say that it is to Le Blond that the present Leningrad owes its greatest street, the Nevsky Prospect.

St Petersburg had been founded in 1703 on a site which had nothing at all to recommend it: at the outlet of the Neva, whose very name in Finnish means mud. The location chosen for the new capital was described as having 'On the one side the sea, on the other sorrow, on the third moss, on the fourth a sigh'. But the all-powerful Peter was determined to have his outlet to the sea, his window to Europe, and cost what it might, the city had to be built.

Then Peter had cast his eye further afield and desired a country palace; Le Blond was to build it for him. A site was chosen eighteen miles out of St Petersburg overlooking the sea, near the mouth of the Neva – with a view towards the coast of Finland, from whence Peter could watch his beloved new navy sail up to his new harbour. The position, for a change, was a promising one, and the new palace was built on a natural rise in the ground, fifty feet high, making at first a sharp, and then a gradual, slope towards the sea. Peter took a hand himself in the design and planning of the palace, and some of his own preliminary sketches exist. Forty thousand trees were planted, mostly the indigenous trees of Russia such as elms, maples and firs: then ship-loads of trees were brought from Europe, and beeches, limes and fruit-trees were induced to take root in the sandy, cheerless soil. They flourished surprisingly; and in spite of cold, two hundred endless Russian winters and the ravages of the last war, many trees of the original planting are still there, and the park at Peterhof today presents a picture of smiling verdure.

Thus the area of the new garden between the terrace and the sea was planted with bosquets in the French manner, intersected by several avenues. At each end of the largest of these stands an enchanting pavilion, Le Blond's legacy, although he did not live to see them completed. One is called Mon Plaisir, built in the Dutch style in rosy brick, and situated right on the water's edge with its windows looking out to sea, towards the Fortress of Kronstadt; beside it lies a neatly kept flower garden. The other pavilion, Marly, has great charm, too, and presents a pleasantly quiet Dutch appearance (Peter had a passion for everything Dutch), dreaming the centuries away among its trees and beside its peaceful lake, where Peter used to summon his pet carp for their evening meal by ringing a handbell.

Nearby is a joke tree-fountain like the one at Chatsworth, called the 'Oak-tree', which spouts water at the unwary visitor. The 6th Duke of Devonshire visited Russia in 1825 to represent King George IV at the coronation of the Tsar Nicholas I, and it is possible that the tree-fountain of Peterhof may have given him the idea of restoring the one in his own garden in far off Derbyshire. The 'Oak-tree' at Peterhof still amuses thousands of visitors to the garden every year, and must have had a special appeal to Peter, with his boisterous sense of humour. This, however, was combined with a strong desire to learn, and a desire to teach as well: after all, he may have felt, 'If I do not learn, how can I teach the millions of my pupils who are the people of Russia?'

An example of this 'educative instinct' is given in Mr Christopher Marsden's absorbing book about early St Petersburg, *Palmyra of the North*. While discussing garden-plans,

> Peter observed in the upper garden, behind the palace, two long squares of lawn which, he thought, should have seats on them and be used for relaxation. 'I am very pleased with the plan and its execution,' he said to the gardener, 'but I should have thought you could have designed, instead of these insignificant bits of grass, something more instructive. What do you think?' 'Well,' replied the gardener, 'the only thing I can think of is to put books on the seats; then we shall have to work out some way of keeping them from getting wet.' 'Wait a minute,' said the Tsar, laughing, 'I've got an idea. Let us put here and there, as one sees at Versailles, hollow lead statues of subjects taken, say, from Aesop's fables! The statues could be gilded and would emit water, each in its own attitude. A statue of Aesop could be placed at the entrance.' These leaden statues were executed mainly by the sculptor Joseph Simon, Pineau's brother-in-law; he and Pineau also did some similar figures for the Summer Garden in the city. The Tsar made sure that their educative value should be appreciated: thinking that, unaided, the works might be above the heads of his promenading subjects, he had a post put up in front of each statue with a tin plate nailed to it, explaining the figure and its moral.

But the glory of the gardens at Peterhof are the stupendous waterworks in front of the palace itself. Here a cascade of foaming water divides on either side of a terraced grotto and falls over six high steps of marble into a basin, which leads in turn to the long canal, stretching, plumed with fountains all the way, towards the sea. Later, two more cascades were added, in one, the Golden Mountain, water gushes down over a glistening flight of golden steps, and in the other, the Chess Board, over squares of black and white marble. The fountains and cascades are given an extraordinary character by the luminous greenish white gleam of the water, a renowned quality of the spring water which comes from the nearby Ropsha Hills. All about stand classical statues of brilliantly gilded bronze, the only ones left in such profusion in any gardens of the world today. These were originally of lead, but were replaced at the end of the eighteenth century by the architect Veronikhin with statues of gilded bronze. In the central pool a golden Samson forces open the jaws of a golden lion, and the jet from the dying animal's golden gullet rises forty feet in the air. This is the most spectacular of Peterhof's fountains and was the work of Nicolas Pineau, a pupil of

Gilded youth

A detail of the Roman fountain

Coysevox, whose work we see at Versailles. It commemorates Peter's victory at Poltava over the Swedes, and was erected on the twenty-fifth anniversary of the battle. The effect of the gilded statues and the ice-green water is extraordinary, and to be found in no other garden in Europe: it is almost overwhelming, and seemed so even in the eighteenth century when the eye, perhaps, was more used to bright colour than ours is today. A French Ambassador, accustomed, certainly, to the dazzle of Versailles, criticized the Russians' lavish use of gold in gardens, and when he first saw the Empress Catherine's palace at Tsarkoye-Selo, remarked that all it needed was a case to protect it in bad weather. But there is something magnificent, one must allow, in all this gold, out-doors, in a country with the rudest climate of Europe.

Le Blond died in Russia in 1719, but his work at Peterhof was carried out to his plans by the Italian Nicolo Michetti who had arrived in Russia in 1718. The palace he had built for Peter was reconstructed and substantially added to by the celebrated Bartolomeo Carlo Rastrelli for Peter's ebullient daughter Elizabeth, who, however, would not allow her father's original house to be pulled down: she had an affection for the place, with its woods and avenues running down to the sea, and often stayed there cooking immense meals for herself in the Dutch kitchens of Mon Plaisir. It was during her reign (1741–62) that the 'Coat of Arms' wing, with its gilded onion-dome, and ogival roof tricked out with gilded laurel fronds, was added to the palace, balancing the church wing on the other side.

The enlarged palace was painted, in typical Russian style, a deep raspberry pink and white, which must have made a happy contrast with the iron roof with its gilded trimmings and burnished domes. It is now a less spectacular cream colour. With Tsarkoye-Selo, Peterhof is the only truly French eighteenth-century garden in Russia. Prior to Peter the Great there were no pleasure grounds, as the rest of Europe understood them: with the advent of Catherine II – that most enlightened mon-

Peterhof, showing Rastrelli's additions and the garden in the eighteenth century

arch – only the latest fashion in garden planning was permissible, so the *jardin anglais* became the rule. Peterhof was fortunate in surviving the change of taste through the following two centuries. However it suffered cruelly in the last war, and the palace was almost entirely wrecked. Most of the trees of the garden were cut down or shattered by gun-fire: all the statues, which the German soldiers thought were made of solid gold, were removed and taken to Germany for melting down. But everything, thanks to the devotion of the Department of Fine Arts of the Ministry of Culture for the Preservation of Monuments in the USSR, and their industry and application, has been restored. One particularly happy recreation is that of the Samson group, most impressive of the garden of Peterhof, by the Russian sculptor V. Simonov. Peter the Great would be pleased with everything he saw, if he could revisit today his 'Versailles-by-the-Sea'.

A nymph of gold tips her urn against a background of Peter the Great's trees

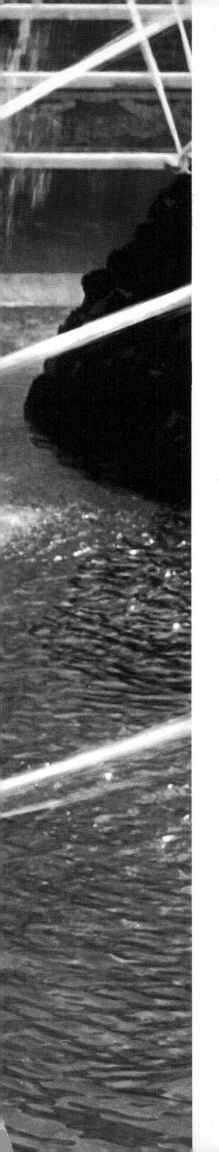

Gilded magnificence and Dutch simplicity

The 'Coat of Arms' wing 'with its gilded onion-dome, and ogival roof tricked out with gilded laurel fronds'

The pavilion of the Hermitage looks over the Bay of Finland

LEFT: *A nereid, merbaby and dolphin in gilded bronze*

Fronteira NEAR LISBON

A fantasy in clipped box and blue tiles

A fountain marbled with orange lichen with the great tank beyond

BIOGRAPHERS OF MARIE ANTOINETTE have often drawn gloomy conclusions from the fact that she was born on November 2nd, All Saints' Day, the Day of the Dead, in 1755, the very day that the great earthquake almost entirely destroyed Lisbon. The earthquake destroyed, as well as the capital, much of the suburb of Bemfica, a leafy village on its outskirts. The pink, pale blue and ochre-painted *quintas* crumbled in a few minutes, and almost the only building to survive was the solidly but elegantly built Quinta de Fronteira, a small palace, then as now, belonging to the Marquis of Fronteira.

Portugal has many ties with far-distant lands. It was occupied for centuries by the Moors, who left their imprint on Portuguese architecture and gardens. It controlled an empire which at different times embraced Brazil, Morocco, parts of India and the Indies. All these influences have coloured Portugal, a country already exotic by its own nature. Its skies are bluer than those of Italy, and its mulberry-coloured earth is richer, and its vegetation more brilliant and varied, than those of any other European country. Lord Byron in *Childe Harold* called it 'a purple land where law secures not life'. Today it is as law-abiding as England, another country with which Portugal has ancient ties.

The garden at Fronteira antedates the better known gardens at Queluz by a century. It is less sophisticated, more robust, less

RIGHT: *'A balustrade of dove-coloured stone'*

French, more Portuguese. Its plan, though it comprises one most unusual feature, is of the simplest, but it has been imbued with a character all its own, a mixture of grandeur and naïveté which is wholly Portuguese.

As in many Portuguese gardens azulejos are a great feature of Fronteira. Azulejos, coloured tiles, are originally said to have been imported from Holland, but later were certainly manufactured in Portugal. They make the beauty of many Portuguese churches and houses as well as gardens; usually blue and white, they are occasionally to be found in other colours, as at the Royal Palace at Queluz, where they are spectacularly employed to depict scenes from Portuguese history, sea-battles and pageants, in pink and yellow, as well as in blue. The earliest tiles were embossed, with the same design reproduced on each tile to give an all-over pattern: later, especially in churches, but more rarely in gardens, panoramic pictures in blue and white, covering large areas of wall, were set up all over Portugal, and as we see, nowhere more effectively than at Fronteira.

Entering the garden, the visitor is confronted with a vast parterre, two hundred and fifty feet square, of meticulously tonsured box, a slow-growing indigenous variety, several hundreds of years old and yet green and thick and full of vigour. Broad paths slice this portion of the garden into four, and each quarter is sub-divided into four again. Where the paths cross, stand graceful fountains and statues. To the right of this formal garden, as exquisitely maintained as any in Europe, lies the sensational feature of Fronteira, a tank: and the word is well chosen, because it is thus that garden pools are called in India, and the

The door to the chapel, flanked with pagan musicians in tile-work. It bears the date 1583

LEFT: *One of the four statues in the tank; on the staircase wall, Neptune in azulejos*

A raised star-shaped lily-pond: beyond lies the tank with the Gallery of Kings above

A garden style which is peculiarly Portugal's

In the Jardin de Venus, a baroque pool lies before the façade of a shell and azulejo decked pavilion

LEFT: *Orpheus from his niche surveys a scene of colour*

tank at Fronteira strongly recalls the East. Along its garden edge is a balustrade of dove-coloured stone, marbled with orange lichen; on either side flights of stairs beckon one up to twin pavilions with pyramidal roofs. The fantasy does not end there. Just under life-size statues, four of them, are placed in the water, their odd proportions making the expanse of water seem wider. Above and beyond the tank runs a terrace adorned with alcoves containing terra-cotta busts of kings and queens of Portugal. This surmounts the further and most remarkable wall of the tank, a wall decorated with fifteen arches, three in the form of recessed grottoes, the other twelve bearing over life-size portraits of twelve knights on horseback. These portraits are executed in blue and white azulejos, and depict the dozen Portuguese heroes who according to legend journeyed to England to avenge the insults offered by the boorish English to twelve Portuguese ladies then visiting their country. Their chivalry is extolled by the great Portuguese poet Camoens in one of the cantos of his poem *The Lusiads*. He describes the knights' reception in England by John of Gaunt, 'time honoured Lancaster', whose daughter Leonora became Queen of Portugal, and from whom the Fronteira family descends. The twelve knights appeared, Camoens informs us:

> With arms and uniforms on latest plan,
> With helmets, crests, devices, gems of art,
> Horses, and all that colour could impart.

The tank in the garden at Fronteira is an astonishing conception and quite unlike anything else in Portugal. Behind it lies an English garden shaded by high trees which afford grateful shade on burning summer days, and under the roof made by their interlacing branches are winding paths with a pool and fountain in the shape of a star at their centre. The walls of the terrace adjoining the palace which leads to the chapel are decorated with more azulejos and wreaths of flowers in the style of Della Robbia. These last were much damaged by Junot's French troops during the Peninsular War.

The azulejos at Fronteira are quite extraordinarily magnificent. Their Delft blue and white makes a perfect contrast with the incandescent geraniums with which the terrace is planted. They form parts of the walls of the balustrading itself, and are further used to make garden benches. It was upon these benches that the guests of one famous occupant of Fronteira must have rested, when the *quinta* was lived in by Donna Leonora d'Almeida in the early nineteenth century. Donna Leonora was a blue stocking, and under the *nom-de-plume* of Alcipe, a writer of note. It is pleasant to think of the erudite and witty hostess, an ardent flower lover, surrounded by her guests in the exquisite gardens of Fronteira, perhaps reading to them her latest and most successful poem, a panegyric on the delights of horticulture.

Wearing the great cross of the Order of Christ: a bust in the Gallery of Portuguese Kings

One of the twelve knights ' with arms and uniforms on latest plan '

LEFT: *A flight of steps rises towards the pavilion with a pyramidal roof*

Villa Garzoni COLLODI, TUSCANY

A Baroque garden with echoes of the Renaissance

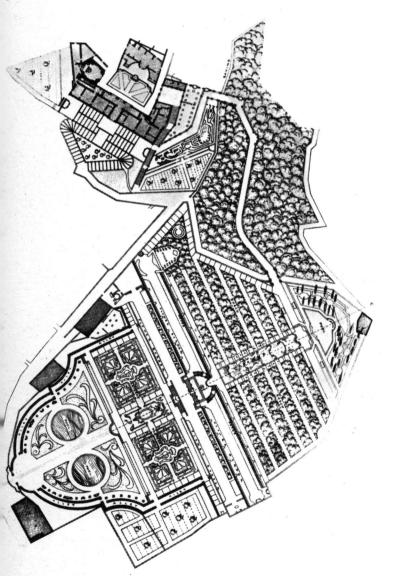

Plan of the garden at Villa Garzoni, Collodi

IT IS DIFFICULT FOR THE VISITOR TO the Villa Garzoni, seeing the garden for the first time, spread down the hillside like a peacock's tail, to withhold a gasp of admiration. The effect is so spectacular, with the twin fountains and the multi-coloured parterre in the foreground, and the triple flight of steps beyond, balustraded and be-niched, climbing to meet the tumbling cascade. Surmounting all, with only some pyramidal cypresses between it and the blue Tuscan sky, is the statue of Fame, which so impressed William Beckford a hundred and eighty years ago:

> Alcina could not have chosen a more romantic situation. The garden lies extended beneath, gay with flowers and glittering with compartments of spar, which . . . has an enchanted effect. Two large marble basins, with *jets-d'eau*, seventy feet in height, divide the parterres, from the extremity of which rises a rude cliff, shaded with firs and ilex and cut into terraces. Leaving our horses at the great gate of this magic enclosure, we passed through the spray of the fountains, and mounting an endless flight of steps, entered an alley of oranges, and gathered ripe fruit from the trees. Whilst we were thus employed, the sun broke from the clouds, and lighted up the green of the vegetation, at the same time spangling the waters, which pour copiously down a succession of rocky terraces, and sprinkle the impending citron-trees with perpetual dew. These streams issue from a chasm in the cliff, surrounded by cypresses, which conceal by their thick branches some pavilions with baths. Above arises a colossal statue of Fame, boldly carved, and in the very act of starting from the precipices. A narrow path leads up to the feet of the goddess, on which I reclined; whilst a vast column of water arching over my head, fell, without even wetting me with its spray, into the depths below.

The gardens of the Villa Garzoni are among the most theatrically magnificent in Italy, and constitute an interesting merger of the Renaissance and baroque styles. Their design is eccentric, for the gardens lie to one side of the villa itself, an arrangement imposed on the original planners in the mid-seventeenth century, by the site. The villa was built on the foundations of an ancient mediaeval fortress, on a high hill-top overlooking the village of Collodi. There was no room for the gardens to spread around: thus they lie at an angle to the villa, an arrangement

RIGHT: *Goat-legged satyrs overlook the terraces*

VILLA GARZONI, COLLODI

Tatterdemalion, in stucco, begs for alms

A satyr overlooking the garden; to the left is a monkey – one of a series – playing pallone

which has the advantage of allowing the occupants of the villa to enjoy from their windows the panorama of the garden's flower-filled terraces.

At the entrance to the garden, great hedges of yew clipped into the shape of towers and battlements stretch to right and left, tunnelled through with shady walks and arbours. On either side lie *broderies* of low box hedges planted with flowers, and a broad gravelled path leads between twin circular *bassins*, with high plume-like fountains, to the main parterre which is outlined with bold yew hedges and studded at the four corners with giant steely-leaved aloes. The whole 'carpet' is intricately planted with succulents, in a complicated pattern of grey, olive green, scarlet and terra-cotta, centering on a vast circle containing the letter G for Garzoni, the family who has owned and maintained the gardens since the late seventeenth century.

Beyond the parterre rise the terrace walls with their surfaces decorated with designs in pebble-work, which recall the Grotto of Pan at Marlia. Balustraded steps lead upward to three great terraces, each embellished with lemon trees in pots, towering palm-trees, and the topmost one with high urn-capped terms with figures of goat-shanked, wily satyrs. An attractive feature of this part of the garden is the monkeys in terra-cotta which caper on the balustrades, playing the game of *pallone*, a sort of football.

Above the third terrace, with steps on either side of it, is the cascade; rough stones, mossy, grass-grown and ferny, border it on either side. As it tumbles down the steep slope it catches the sunbeams and splashes between the grotesque birds which flank it, spouting water. At the top, are typical Tuscan conceits – we see much the same at Marlia – two reclining giant figures symbolizing the cities of Florence and Lucca. High up above, with swollen cheeks and bosom, Fame blows her trumpet and emits the jet of water which passes high over our heads, as it did over Beckford's, to mingle with the cascade below.

There is also, at the Villa Garzoni, an attractive *Teatro di Verdura*, recalling that at Marlia, and a bath-house, charmingly arranged with baths of marble and dressing-rooms, decorated throughout in white, blue and gold, with wall paintings of *Putti* carrying wreaths of flowers.

Although only a few miles apart, and in some superficial details similar (pebble-work, carving, the open-air theatre), the two gardens near Lucca that we have chosen to illustrate in this book could not be more different. At Marlia the effect is achieved by an enfilade of sky-ceiled rooms, walled in hedge, each with an intimacy of its own. Villa Garzoni is a fine example of a baroque garden, like the great gardens of Rome, where the whole design is proudly, and in one splendid flourish, made plain. It is truly magnificent, even pompous. In the late seventeenth century, Francesco Smarra, Court poet to the Emperor Ludwig of Austria, wrote a poem called *The Pomps of Collodi*; and well he might.

RIGHT: *The garden spreads down the hill-side like a peacock's tail*

The strong pattern made by differing plant forms

A boldly patterned garden on a Tuscan hill-side

Fame's jet falls into a pool which feeds the Villa's high cascade

*'High up above, with swollen cheeks and bosom,
Fame blows her trumpet . . .'*

LEFT: *The elaborate pattern of the garden below the terraces*

117

Schwetzingen MANNHEIM
A German garden in the grand manner

THE MANY MINOR POTENTATES, Princes, Dukes, Margraves, of the Holy Roman Empire (which Voltaire dismissed as being neither Holy, Roman nor an Empire), were all great builders and patrons of the arts: as were those other rulers who wielded spiritual as well as temporal power, the Prince Bishops. In fact, most are more clearly remembered, if remembered at all, for their architectural adventures than for their government; for their palaces rather than their policies. What, for instance, do we recall of the achievements of Augustus the Strong of Saxony except that he built the Zwinger Palace in Dresden? Or of the sermons of the Prince Bishops of Würzburg except that they had that beautiful garden at Veitshöchheim to compose them in?

Such a ruler, certainly, was the Elector Palatine Carl Theodor, creator of the garden at Schwetzingen, whose long life bridged the whole era of eighteenth-century enlightenment, being born in 1724 and living long enough to sign a disadvantageous treaty with Revolutionary France in 1797. He came of a cultured and enlightened family. The Elector Johann-Wilhelm, whose brother he succeeded, married Maria Louisa de Medici, whose family founded the Uffizi Gallery. Carl Theodor became Elector in 1742, and Mannheim was his capital until 1778 when, after his succession to the Electorate of Bavaria, it was changed to Munich. This put a curb on building operations and garden developments at Schwetzingen, and brought distress and loss of revenue to Mannheim. Thenceforward Carl Theodor lived in Munich. Though his politics were obscure, unsuccessful and now forgotten, his cultural legacies are important: he initiated the *Academy of Drawing* in Mannheim, of which the great Verschaffelt, designer of the Angel that surmounts the Castel St Angelo in Rome, and sculptor of the noble pair of stags at Schwetzingen, was the first director. The magnificent collection of pictures he brought with him to Munich (well might Mannheim mourn) was the nucleus from which the great collection in the Alte Pinakothek grew: and he was the creator of two of the most charming gardens and parks in Germany,

Gilded 'suns in splendour' shine from the exquisite iron balustrade of the Temple of Apollo

LEFT: *The eighteenth-century wing of the Schloss seen across a bed of wallflowers*

SCHWETZINGEN

The Elector Carl Theodor of Rhineland-Palatinate (1724–99), creator of the garden at Schwetzingen

the *Englischer Garten* in Munich, and those of Schwetzingen itself.

Schwetzingen is a garden of transition, and came into being at a time when the formal garden, gardens such as Vaux and Versailles, were being threatened by the new fashion, which originated, like so many vaguely revolutionary ideas, in England. When the new fashion reached the Continent, there was at first an effort at compromise. Surely the work of years – the high shaven hedges, the elaborate *broderies* of flowers, the sculpted trees, the rigid terraces, were not all to be swept away overnight? Must they immediately be replaced with 'natural' features such as the winding path and bosky grove? Finally, surrender to the new style was unconditional and complete, and the idea of the landscape garden, as first evolved at Stourhead, spread all over the Continent, sweeping away many exquisite earlier gardens in its train. Schwetzingen, however, is a rare example of successful compromise. It was first laid out for the Elector Carl Theodor in the old formal French style by the architect Nicolas Pigage with the assistance of a head gardener, Petrini, about 1753. The Bible of French garden art *La Théorie et Pratique du Jardinage*, was closely consulted in its planning. This remarkable book, which had the greatest influence on garden planners who sought to emulate French models, first appeared anonymously in France in 1709, although the author was said to be Alexandre Jean-Baptiste Le Blond who had worked

An early Victorian print of the Fountain of the Birds which has changed little with the years

at Versailles and was invited to Russia by Peter the Great to design the garden at Peterhof in 1716. No previous book had expounded so clearly the principles of garden planning, nor had so exclusively concerned itself with the pleasure garden. It dismissed the *potager* as uninteresting and unlovely (would that Le Blond could see the vegetable garden at Villandry) but expected the aspiring garden architect to be a man of parts:

Plan of the garden before Von Skell's alterations

> He must be something of a geometrician, must understand architecture, must be able to draw well, must know the character and effect of every plant he makes use of for fine gardens, and must also know the art of ornament. He must be inventive, and above all intelligent: he must have a natural good taste cultivated by the sight of beautiful objects and the criticism of ugly ones, and must have an all-round interest and insight in these matters.

A glance at the plan of the Schwetzingen garden will show that it was of the greatest complexity. The parterres, first circular, and then in giant rectangles stretched, as at Versailles, towards a *tapis vert*, which divided – again as at Versailles – twin bosquets, and was lined on either side with statues. The *tapis vert* was traversed by a canal which widened a little at the point of intersection: what is unusual at Schwetzingen was the graceful way in which the semi-circular lines of trellises which bordered the first parterre were built to continue the line of the galleries of the château, so making a full circle. This gives the gardens great individuality. Furthermore, unlike the great par-

Symbols of Schwetzingen are this pair of white stags, sculpted by Peter von Verschaffelt

the garden of Schwetzingen

LEFT: *A well muffled statue of Winter in a leafy frame*

EXTREME LEFT: *Simon Lamine's statue of Pan in an Arcadian setting*

BELOW: *The seventeenth-century Schloss of Schwetzingen; in the foreground, a classic urn*

An obelisk and a rustic belvedere in a setting of ornamental ruins

The pink-painted colonnade, which adjoins the Mosque, looks onto beds of coloured flowers

terres of France, which always lay open, in all their embroidered elaboration, to the sky, those at Schwetzingen were intersected, lengthways and across, by avenues of small trees. These, though kept small by clipping, provided shade and a degree of privacy which were to the taste of the smaller German Courts. This was the picture that the gardens presented two hundred years ago: today the trees have grown and the effect, though still very beautiful, is completely changed.

Thus, in its most important lines, the garden at Schwetzingen derived from France. Carl Theodor further adorned it with a series of charming *fabriques* or follies or garden-features, call them what one may. Pigage designed a delicious *Théâtre de Verdure*, which recalls the temporary one created at Vaux for Fouquet's famous fête, and the theatre of living green which still graces the garden at Marlia. Pigage's theatre has for background a domed Temple of Apollo, in which, left-handed, the god plays his lyre. Nearby is his delightful bath-pavilion (1766), probably inspired by the Badenburg at Nymphenburg, built some years before it. It is here that the visitor to Schwetzingen experiences one of its most charming conceits, the Fountain of the Birds. It depicts in bronze the story of the owl who killed another bird, and in punishment has water squirted at him for evermore by all the other birds of the world. And there he is – prey in claw – but sadly dishevelled by the watery revenge of his feathered enemies. This delightful work was brought to Schwetzingen from Lunéville where Nicolas Pigage had been Court architect. There were other delightful features of the garden at Schwetzingen, sculpture, temples and fountains all in the traditional French taste, but the whole elaborate and intricate layout, with its toys and fancies were mostly swept away when Carl Theodor became influenced by the new ideas from England, and started to hanker for a garden in the new fashionable natural style. But fortunately Ludwig von Skell, the first landscape gardener in Germany, who visited England in 1776 and had seen much of what was happening there, had the good sense to refuse to destroy Pigage's garden to suit the new mode. Instead, as can be seen from a second plan of the gardens at Schwetzingen, he confined himself to altering the outer parts of the garden, romanticizing the stiff lines of the Canal – now renamed Der See – but leaving the older formal parterres intact. But his additions met with the disapproval of Christian Hirschfeld, who in 1771 had published a paper on botany, which was followed in 1779 by his great work in five volumes, *The History and Theory of Horticulture*. The first expert on the subject in Germany, he considered himself the champion of garden good taste in the Fatherland. Even Goethe said of him, 'He lit with his own fire the emulation and enthusiasm of others'. Hirschfeld visited the garden in 1784 and hated all he saw. Von Skell was in the process of planting an English park, which he chose, perilously close to the original French parterre, to adorn with a Mosque. 'Look at the Mecca scene, for example,' cried Hirschfeld, his German *Geschmack* outraged. 'This Mecca in the middle of the French part . . . this monument ought not, if the illusion is to be preserved, to be very different from ruins which are nearly worn away by the hand of time: but here everything is new, perfect, ornate.'

Neither did Von Skell's attempts at an English garden meet with the approval of that well-known dilettante William Beckford who also visited Schwetzingen, and wrote:

Not many leagues out of town lie the famous gardens of Schweidsing. The weather being extremely warm, we were glad to avail ourselves of their shades. There are a great many fountains enclosed by thickets of shrubs and cool alleys which led to arbours of trellis work, festooned with nasturtiums and convolvulus . . . the song of exotic birds; the freshness of the surrounding verdure heightened by falling streams; and that dubious poetic light admitted through thick foliage – so agreeable after the glare of a sultry day, detained me for some time in an alcove reading Spenser. . . . I would fain have loitered an hour more, in this enchanted bower, had not the gardener, whose patience was quite exhausted . . . dragged me away to a sunburnt contemptible hillock . . . decorated with the title of *Jardin anglois*. A glance was all I bestowed on this caricature upon English gardens: I then went off in a huff at being chased from my bower and grumbled all the road to Entsweigen, where, to our misfortune, we lay, amidst hogs and vermin, who amply revenged my quarrels with their country.

Von Skell's essay at an English garden, and his addition of a mosque, imposing and effective as it is, may not be his happiest creation, but his conjuring of Der See, with its romantic inlets and promontories, is wholly successful.

Today, the gardens of Schwetzingen, scented with the lilacs for which they are famous, with their lawns dotted with peacocks and the sun glancing down through the lime tree leaves, present a beautiful picture in early summer, and transport the visitor from bustling, prosperous Western Germany to the sunlit grace of another age.

After the transfer of the capital from Mannheim to Munich, work went on, desultorily, on the gardens, but the impetus was gone. Von Skell's most famous work was the *Englischer Garten* in Munich. Carl Theodor, now Elector of Palatinate-Bavaria, lived on, still designing gardens and building palaces, a typical Prince of the eighteenth century. He was born within a few years of Madame de Pompadour, lived through the baroque age, and into the age of rococo. He saw the artifices of the Ancien Régime blown away by the no less artificially contrived gusts of the Romantic Revival. As already recorded, one of his last acts was to sign the Peace of Campo Formio, by which he lost the left bank of the Rhine, with the young French Republic. The new century was now at the door, and the time for Carl Theodor to plan gardens and build palaces was over. He died in the last year of the eighteenth century.

The Mosque built about 1780 by Nicolas Pigage, which so aroused Hirschfeld's disapproval

Chatsworth DERBYSHIRE

The garden of England's finest country house

Kip engraving of Kniff's 'perspective', published in the 'Nouveau Théâtre de la Bretagne', 1716

The Sea Horse fountain: Cibber sculpted the figures

THERE ARE SOME, BUT VERY FEW, HOUSES whose very names have a special magic. Chatsworth is one: it evokes grandeur, spells something remote, suggests the unattainable. And yet Chatsworth has never been, as other great English country houses have been, the scene of great events: indeed, as its story unfolds, it seems as if history has almost passed it by.

The house – one of the many great houses owned by the Dukes of Devonshire – lies in one of the most beautiful and rugged parts of Derbyshire. Its bland façades of golden sandstone, carved, as Horace Walpole found, 'with the neatness of wrought plate', look over a rolling park, the pasturage of deer. All around are tree-clad hills, making a cradle for the house to dream in, aloof, detached from time.

The shade of Mary Queen of Scots pervades the park, for she was imprisoned in a house on the same site. The final tragedy happened at Fotheringhay, eighty miles away, but legends of her baleful beauty linger. In the Civil War, the original house, as many did, changed hands more than once, and Royalists and Roundheads held it in succession; yet when the owner returned from the Continent, where owing to his Royalist sympathies he prudently retired, he found his property but little damaged.

The first Duke won his dukedom, not for his loyalty to James II, but for his eager acceptance of William III. The second Duke

RIGHT: *The parterre below the west façade planted in box to reproduce the ground plan of Chiswick House*

'*New statues were ordered to replace Cibber's . . . from Carrara . . .*'

was distinguished for his 'dogged veracity' rather than for more spectacular abilities. His son achieved the Premiership – but only for eight months. The fifth Duke's greatest claim to fame is that his wife was the legendary Georgiana; but it was London which saw the 'face without a frown' more often than Derbyshire.

A mild fame, it is true, invested Chatsworth when the sixth Duke built there the biggest greenhouse in the world. It was he who added greatly to Chatsworth's prestige; and as his building progressed, and the gardens spread, the legend grew. When he inherited in 1811 there were few notable works of art at Chatsworth: he died leaving it a treasure house. All through the nineteenth century the house's fame increased, and it became a centre of entertaining on a vast scale. Queen Victoria and other crowned heads were visitors, and it was in the Victorian and Edwardian age that Chatsworth achieved its eminence as the first of English country houses. Yet there was never a Chatsworth set, Cabinets were not formed there; it was the house itself that achieved fame rather than its occupants. A politically-minded Duke of Devonshire, the eighth, became Secretary of State for India, and was offered, but declined the Premiership; another became Governor General of Canada, and doubtless dreamed, as he looked at the St Lawrence, of the Derwent River and the pheasant coverts of home. His grandson married Kathleen Kennedy, sister of the President, and died in 1944, fighting in Belgium. The present Duke, on inheriting, was faced with savage death duties: but in spite of these he and his beautiful wife still live in part of the house, and devote their youthful energies, imagination and taste to administering the vast property which is, as it has long been, open to the public and its treasures available for all to enjoy.

The history of the gardens at Chatsworth can roughly be divided into five periods. Of the earliest Elizabethan garden which lay about the Tudor house, little or nothing remain. Of the first Duke's garden, parterred and statued, some fountains, terracing and the celebrated cascade, though enlarged later, survive. The fourth Duke, with Capability Brown's assistance, swept away, in the full flush of the Romantic Revival, most of the first Duke's formal features. The sixth Duke restored some of the vanished formality, and made his own immense additions, in which he was aided by the brilliant Joseph Paxton. Then ensued a long sunlit century when successive duchesses loved and nurtured the garden, which grew, under their care, and that of eighty gardeners, to splendid maturity. Finally today the present reigning couple have devoted imagination and zest to endow the garden, in spite of their reduced resources, with new life.

Sole relic of the Elizabethan garden, which lay round the high, slightly grim, castellated Chatsworth of the day, are the Hunting Tower and Queen Mary's Bower. Though much restored, most of the masonry of the last is Elizabethan, and the miniature fortress, set in a moat, presents a most romantic picture, and may well have been used as an agreeable and secure summer-house for the unfortunate Scottish Queen during her detention. 'Suffer ye Quene,' advises Cecil in a letter which still exists, 'to take ye ayre about your howse . . .', and it is here that she may well have done so, in her flowery but high-walled bower, wafting messages, as Schiller suggests she did, on the clouds sailing overhead, to her beloved France.

By the last quarter of the next century the garden at Chatsworth had been greatly developed. As soon as the political upheavals of the Revolution in 1688 calmed down, the first Duke embarked on many garden projects. Soon the Elizabethan house had made way for the classical, almost baroque, building we see today. Of the garden of that time, Mr Francis Thompson, in his comprehensive *History of Chatsworth*, writes:

> In those days, abstract 'Nature' did not count. In the Duke's eyes and in those of his contemporaries, a classical building required a classical setting; and this setting it was the function of the garden to provide. Fifty years or more were to pass before the contrast between a formal garden and the ruggedness of the surrounding landscape began to appear objectionable. The Duke, on the contrary, welcomed the contrast, and sought to emphasise it in every conceivable way; Kniff's drawing, which illustrates the stage reached in 1699, is the best possible index both of the purpose of the first Duke's garden and of the success with which it answered this purpose.

The house was set in a system of terraces, decorated with statues by the Danish sculptor, Caius Cibber, who had studied in Rome, and had come to England at the Restoration. George London, of the London firm of London and Wise, laid out the west parterre, following the precepts laid down in their own popular work *The Compleat Gardener*. As gardeners, they were highly praised by John Evelyn, the diarist, for their 'industry, knowledge of nature and genius of soils'. Wise was afterwards gardener to Queen Anne.

The Emperor fountain, with the highest jet in England, was built to honour the visit of the Tsar of Russia

Chatsworth: the west front

CHATSWORTH

The view towards the house from the Cascade House

Following the completion of the west parterre, work on the south parterre followed, and a vast project, which entailed the levelling of a sizeable hill was carried out. This completely altered the lie of the land to the south and south-west of the house, and opened up the splendid view which can today be enjoyed from the terraces.

It was at this time that advantage was first taken of the enormous high-level supply of water which made possible the Cascade and lofty fountains which were soon to make the fame of the garden of Chatsworth. A Frenchman, Grillet, was in charge of these new waterworks, which at the time and for many years were considered sensational. Indeed, as Mr Thompson writes:

> The waterworks were the chief note of the first Duke's garden. Whether in the form of ponds or of mere fountains, there was water everywhere. The total area of water, in relation to the size of the whole garden, must have been enormous. Of the fountains, nine (excluding those connected with the Cascade) are mentioned by name in the accounts: the Venus fountain, the Boreas fountain, the Neptune fountain, the Triton fountain, the Willow Tree fountain, the Sea Horse fountain, the fountain in the new garden (the west parterre), the Greenhouse fountain, and the fountain in the Canodire (that is, the duck-decoy at the south end of the Canal Pond); but there were no doubt many lesser ones. An underground network of pipes and streams survives (as the gardeners know to their cost in rainy weather) to this day, although the fountains themselves have mostly vanished.

Six years before Anne's succession in 1702, the most sensational of all the waterworks at Chatsworth was completed, the Cascade, with its fascinating Cascade House, said to be the work of the architect Thomas Archer. This is a most elegant building: water gushes down the roof, from high set basins and from the mouths of vomiting dolphins carved, in high relief, on its façade of rusticated stone. To add to the flow of water, a new pond was dug above and plans laid for the water to fall from the very summit of the hill behind, which that inveterate country-house visitor, Celia Fiennes, thought would greatly 'add to the curiositye'.

Of all these water-wonders only the Cascade, the Sea Horse fountain and the Triton fountain survive: the delightful and slightly ridiculous Willow Tree fountain -- a tree in copper – which spouts water from its leaves over the unwary visitor, is a reproduction. All the rest were swept away by the change of fashion, which affected Chatsworth just as it did Schwetzingen, and hundreds of other gardens in England and on the Continent in the mid-eighteenth century: the Romantic Revival.

Mr Thompson points out that it was the fourth Duke (1720–64) who created the modern Chatsworth, and gave the whole domain its present character. His reign as Duke was short, only eight years, and he was more involved in public life than his predecessors and successors and, perhaps more important, he married the greatest heiress of the day, the daughter of the architect Earl of Burlington, who certainly must have influenced his taste.

The gardens were entirely re-orientated. The statues and parterres to the west of the house were abolished, leaving only two great pedestals carved with trophies of arms and bearing Cibber's sphinxes. The park swept up to the very walls of the house. Horace Walpole, in general, regretted the changes, but there is good garden sense in his criticism when he writes: 'The great *jet d'eau* I like, nor would I remove it; whatever is magnificent of the kind in the time it was done I would retain, else all houses and gardens wear a tiresome resemblance. I except that absurdity of a cascade tumbling down marble steps, which reduces the steps to be of no use at all.' Mr Thompson writes: 'Here it will be noticed, his views were directly at variance with the Duke's; what the Duke was destroying, Walpole would have preserved, and the one characteristic feature of the old garden which the Duke had decided to preserve, Walpole would have destroyed. About the Cascade some modern critics might agree with him.' Some years later, however, Walpole changed his mind: 'Chatsworth,' he wrote, 'I had seen it before, but it is much improved by the late Duke, many foolish waterworks being taken away, oaks and rocks taken into the garden and a magnificent bridge built.'

Walpole, a late apostle of the Romantic Movement, had come round to the changes wrought by the fourth Duke with the aid of Lancelot Brown, high priest, inventor after Henry Hoare of Stourhead, of the natural style. In Capability Brown's view, as Mr Thompson writes:

> The gardens were no longer treated primarily as a setting for the house, but as an extension, however tamed and, so to speak, ducalized, of the natural features of the surrounding landscape. In the immediate neighbourhood of the building the notes of order and formality were maintained, as they are still; but outside this comparatively restricted range the effect aimed at was simply one of rugged grandeur. The fountains, all but a few, were demolished; the symmetrical terraces were smoothed into irregular slopes; the old parterres gave way to landscape and rockwork, at first on a small but later on a colossal scale; the ordered lines of fruit-trees and the old groves of fir and holly and clipped yew arranged in geometric patterns were dug up, and their place taken by forest-trees disposed singly or in random groups; flower-beds were converted into lawns; colour was reduced in tone, if not altogether banished.

Changes were also made at this time to the park, where new roads were laid, and a new bridge built by Paine to span the River Derwent.

The fourth Duke, under whom the garden at Chatsworth took on the appearance it has today, died in 1764, and there followed a lull in gardening operations for nearly fifty years. The fifth Duke, husband of the famous Georgiana, does not seem to have taken a great interest in the gardens, which seem about to have reverted to nature to a greater extent, owing to neglect, perhaps

The Cascade House, said to be the work of Thomas Archer

CHATSWORTH

than even Capability Brown, advocate of assimilation between garden and surrounding landscape, would have wished. No trace of the first Duke's elaborate parterres remained: deer grazed on them, and only in very dry weather were their outlines visible in the turf, as they occasionally are today.

In 1811, the sixth Duke succeeded on reaching the age of twenty-one. He was to live and die a bachelor, and he never held high office; his time, and his heart, were to be devoted to Chatsworth. First the house, which he enormously enlarged and rearranged, was chief object of his attentions: then, in 1826, he met Joseph Paxton, and it was the gardens that were touched with a magician's wand.

Joseph Paxton (1801–65), whose name will ever be linked with that of the sixth Duke, was of simple origin. His path crossed that of his future patron when he was working for 18s. a week at the Royal Horticultural Society garden which, at that time, adjoined Chiswick House, near London, which had come to the Devonshires through the Burlington marriage. Impressed by Paxton's imagination and industry, the Duke offered him the position of superintendent of the gardens at Chatsworth. Thereafter Paxton's career was meteoric: fifteen years later he was recognized as one of Britain's leading horticulturalists, and had built the world's largest greenhouse: a few more years and he had designed the fabulous Crystal Palace, and was knighted.

It was Paxton who kindled the sixth Duke's interest in the garden and furthermore the plants at Chatsworth. Together they evolved and carried out a plan which was a happy compromise between the old formality and the now less fashionable return to Nature. The Duke had, up till then, treated the gardens as an important adjunct to the house – no more: Paxton introduced him to the delights and fascinations of horticulture. 'Not till 1832,' the Duke records, 'did I take to caring for my plants in earnest.'

Plantations were extended, and groves of rhododendrons planted, terraces were rehabilitated, lawns re-laid. New statues

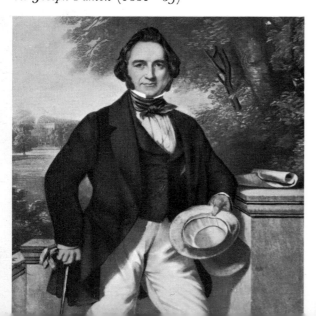

Sir Joseph Paxton (1801–65)

It involved great cost and labour to erect the rocks

to replace Cibber's, long since ravaged by the harsh climate of Derbyshire, were ordered from Francesco Bienaimé of Carrara, whom we meet at Marlia, when he was brought to Italy from Paris by Elisa Baciocchi to revive the Carrara marble industry. Fragments of a Greek temple were shipped from Sunium; new trees clothed the surrounding hills, ingeniously planted in wedge-shaped stands, so that as they matured and were cut the younger trees behind became visible, and thus the felling seemed less drastic. Exotic trees filled the arboretum, classed according to the several natural orders of Jussieu, whom we see at work for Louis XV and Madame de Pompadour at Versailles: each name was printed on small upright boards, which may have borne some resemblance to head-stones, for an unhorticulturally minded French visitor once exclaimed, 'Que c'est touchant ... ce sont les tombeaux de plantes'.

One garden feature which was retained and refurbished, near the new plantings of rare conifers, was Duchess Georgiana's underground grotto of which the walls glittered, and still do, with crystals of copper-ore from the mines of Ecton in Staffordshire. Three of the great sights of the Chatsworth garden which date from Paxton's reign and which were the wonder of visitors, were the great rocks, the Queen's, Prince Albert's and, grandest of all, the Duke of Wellington's, which were moved into the grounds by Paxton for their romantic effect: transporting and erecting them involved immense labour and expense, but the complicated arrangements were just what Paxton excelled at. 'The spirit of some Druid,' the Duke wrote admiringly, 'seems to animate Mr Paxton in these bulky removals.'

But the greatest wonder of all was, of course, the greenhouse, the 'great stove', built in 1836–41. The sixth Duke writes of it thus:

> You arrive at the great Conservatory. It is not a thing to be described, and all my attempts will be to enable you to see, and make others see, what it contains, with the least fatigue and trouble. Its success has been complete, both for the growth of plants and the enjoyment it

The bridge over the river Derwent, completed in 1762

The Wellington rock, 'the spirit of some druid', wrote the sixth Duke admiringly, 'seems to animate Mr Paxton in these bulky removals'

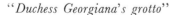
"Duchess Georgiana's grotto"

affords, being, I believe, the only hothouse known to remain, in which longer than ten minutes does not produce a state of suffering. In consequence also of the subterranean furnaces, to which a railway conducts the coal, there is the remarkable feature of cleanliness, and absence of smoke and smell, unknown in any other building of the kind.

And he went on to say, like a kindly and satisfied host,

It never seems to disappoint anybody, and to excite something like enthusiasm in all.

The 'great stove', where *Musa cavendishii*, a variety of banana, first fruited in England, and the Lily House, in which was housed the giant Victoria Regia Lily, which is also grown at the Villa Taranto, survived, the admiration of all, until the First World War, during which its pampered occupants died from lack of heat. The ninth Duke decided to dismantle them, or rather, blow them up. It was probably necessary, but a great pity, especially as twenty years later Paxton's other masterpiece, the Crystal Palace, was destroyed by fire.

The sixth Duke, who had done so much for the fame of Chatsworth, died in 1858; Paxton in 1865. They are both buried in nearby Edensor. For more than a century, through two world wars, the gardens remained much as they left them, Duchess Evelyn, wife of the ninth Duke, being specially active in their

The new serpentine hedge of beech

A contemporary photograph of Paxton's great conservatory, built in 1836–41

Paxton's 'conservative wall' is still in use

care and embellishment. It was she who moved to Chatsworth the many fine pieces of statuary from Chiswick House. Fewer gardeners and changing times have done remarkably little to alter their character.

The present Duke and Duchess of Devonshire have brought their very special gifts of imagination and what can only, admiringly, be called *fantaisie* to Chatsworth. The garden and park are meticulously kept; and the house and grounds are visited by thousands every year (a quarter of a million in 1961) which contributes substantially to their upkeep. The small sum each visitor pays buys endless treats: not only the house, with its untold art treasures, but the gardens, grown to their magnificent prime and now rejuvenated by several touches devised by the present Duchess, the possessor of great beauty and a sprightly imagination. The serpentine hedge of beech, for instance, which continues the axis running from the rose garden to the Sunium pillar, the new maze planted on the site of Paxton's great stove (who else in England would plant a maze today?) and brightest touch of all, the planting of the lawn below the west façade in a design of box exactly reproducing the ground plan of Chiswick House.

Chatsworth has often been happy in its owners: but never happier than now.

An aerial view of Chatsworth

Stourhead WILTSHIRE

The first landscape garden in Europe

The lake with its bridge and temples: From an eighteenth-century print

IT HAS BEEN SAID THAT England's only unique contribution to the world of art is the invention of the landscape garden, and in particular the English park; of this Stourhead in Wiltshire is a supreme example.

Stourhead is situated in the green and hilly south-west corner of Salisbury Plain. It was here, in the early eighteenth century, that Henry Hoare, of the well-known banking family, built a handsome house. Colin Campbell was his architect, and the date was 1714, the year of King George I's accession. The new house was in the fashionable Palladian style, but Henry Hoare did not live long to enjoy it, for in 1725 he was succeeded by his son, the second Henry, and creator of the superb landscape garden that we admire today, two-and-a-half centuries later.

The name Stourhead derives from the house's site, near the headwaters of the River Stour, the river which was dammed to make the lake which is the central and most important feature of the landscape garden. It is likely that work on the garden was started by the younger Henry about 1740, after the death of his mother, who lived on at Stourhead in her widowhood. Whatever the exact date, it was certainly the first English landscape garden; Lancelot Brown did not start work on any scale till 1750, and Uvedale Price, a great admirer and emulator of Henry Hoare, till forty years later. The only essays in landscape

136

RIGHT: '*A magnificent replica, en petit, of the Pantheon in Rome*' built by Henry Flitcroft in about 1745

Neptune, by Rysbrack, tips his urn

The grotto. 'Here, on a watery couch, reclines the nymph . . .'

LEFT: *'The eye is led away over the waters of the lake . . .'*

gardening before Stourhead are the formal avenues that we see in Kip's views, with their geometric plantings inspired by such gardens as Versailles and Vaux-le-Vicomte.

Henry Hoare must surely have been a man of outstanding foresight and taste. But to envisage the garden at Stourhead, to imagine the valley filled with water, the bare downs clothed with woods, and the newly created landscape set with temples and grottoes, as in fact Henry Hoare must have done, calls for imaginative and inventive genius of the highest quality. We must remember that in 1740 it had never been done before: 'landscape-gardener' was a term that did not exist, and the romantic, natural garden was as yet unthought of. By damming up two valleys, Henry Hoare created a lake of over twenty acres; the banks he planted with fir and beech trees. Over the years many of the firs have died or been cut down, leaving the beeches to rear their silver trunks in sole splendour. They are now over two hundred years old and in full maturity. Their towering architecture ennobles the scene, and has the effect of making the lakeside banks seem steeper than they are.

Stourhead has always been an attraction for travellers; and to accommodate sightseers an inn, which still exists, was built on the eastern confines of the grounds. From there, suitably refreshed, the visitor may start his tour by making his way towards the lake. As it comes into view, in spring, spanned by a five-arched bridge, embosomed in trees of every shade of green from the sombre shades of the remaining firs to the sharp young green of beech leaves, the lake presents a landscape of amazing beauty; it might have been painted by Poussin. The eye is led away over the waters of the lake to a succession of further views and vistas, paler and more misty as they recede, giving an impression of going on, like a dream, for ever: such was the art of Henry Hoare.

Bearing right, we pass the Temple of Flora with its elegant pillared and pedimented façade of golden stone against a leafy curtain of trees. Walking beside the lake, with the branches of beech trees high above and the colour, in early summer, of masses of rhododendrons and later of hydrangeas all around, we then approach the most remarkable and dramatic of the 'features' of the garden at Stourhead – the grotto, which still retains, in this prosaic age, something of the mysterious and romantic atmosphere that it must have had when Pope's famous grotto at Twickenham inspired it. Steep steps, between moss-upholstered rocks, lead down to a subterranean cavern, round and vaulted and lit dramatically from above. To one side is an alcove of rusticated stone and shells: here, on a watery couch, reclines the Nymph of the Grot, cast in lead by Rysbrack, and charming in her clinging draperies. One of the springs which

STOURHEAD

feeds the River Stour flows from the wall behind her, and falls into an inky pool below. One of the three great stones which border it is inscribed with some lines by Pope:

Nymph of the Grot, these sacred springs I keep
And to the murmur of these waters sleep.
Ah, spare my slumbers, gently tread the cave
And drink in silence, or in silence, lave.

Sparing the Nymph's repose, we tip-toe on, past another fine statue by Rysbrack, of Neptune emptying an urn from which gushes yet another spring.

Out into the sunshine once more, we pass the head of the lake and bear round by the other side. Here the path leads us by way of, first, a rustic cottage, and beyond, a soaring grove of cypresses underplanted with azaleas, a magnificent replica, *en petit*, of the Pantheon in Rome. Though small in scale, this is still a most imposing building, dating from about 1745, with a classic portico of finely carved pillars and an interior consisting of a high rotunda decorated with statues, including yet more works of Rysbrack – a sturdy Hercules and engaging Flora, as well as some terra-cotta plaques of classic scenes.

Continuing our way, we pass a Temple of the Sun, said to be modelled on one at Baalbec, and so come to the bridge which was in the foreground of the picture when we had our first glimpse of the lake and its summer woods. Having crossed it, we complete the circuit and mount the slope that leads back to the house, passing on the way the curious cross, brought to Stourhead from Bristol where it was lying, in pieces and neglected, in 1768. It dates from 1373 and is one of the best preserved of all English market crosses.

These short notes on the garden at Stourhead are in part inspired by the drawings of a Swedish visitor in 1779, Fredrik Magnus Piper, which add much to our knowledge of the garden, giving a clear idea of how they looked in their first twenty-five years of existence, before the trees had grown to their full splendour that we see today.

One attraction at Stourhead that Piper depicted – it may be the kind of parasol that appears in the foreground of one of the drawings – was an exotic looking 'Turkish Tent'. This was much admired by a visitor to Stourhead in 1776, Mrs Lybbe Powys, who wrote enthusiastically: 'The Turkish Tent at Mr Hoare's is very pretty; 'tis of painted canvas, so remains up the whole year; the inside painted blue and white in mosaic.'

It is sad that, when so much survives, this charmingly frivolous adornment of the grounds at Stourhead should have disappeared.

The market cross, brought from Bristol in 1768, dates from 1373

The Temple of the Sun, said to be modelled on one at Baalbec, with a view across the lake towards the Temple of Flora

A temple,
a bridge and
a cottage orné

'The path leads us by way of a rustic cottage . . .'

The lake at Stourhead

Veitshöchheim NEAR WÜRZBURG

The most enchanting garden statuary in Europe

A FEW MILES FROM WÜRZBURG lies what used to be one of the country palaces of the Prince Bishops of that city, Veitshöchheim, called after St Veit, the patron saint of the region. Its gardens are of far more interest than the rather modest Schloss; for they breathe the very air of the eighteenth century, and to visit them is like being invited to take part in a private revel of the rococo.

Bavaria, with Austria, was fertile ground for the seeds of the baroque and rococo, those two styles, one springing from the other, which are so often quite misunderstood in England and America, and even in France. The Oxford Dictionary defines baroque as 'grotesque', while rococo it dismisses as 'tastelessly florid' or 'fantastic'. The dividing line between the two styles is difficult to fix, but one could say that baroque architecture, high-spirited, elaborate and grand, had its origin in Italy in the second half of the seventeenth century, and lasted for over a century, giving birth, half-way through its long life in about 1730, to rococo, a word which stems from *rocaille*, but which has come to mean a style which is generally gayer, more sophisticated and lighter than its more ponderous parent.

Though finding its most spectacular form in the architecture of palaces like Sans Souci, and monasteries like Ettal or Wies, rococo was a style eagerly welcomed by garden planners of the eighteenth century. It was exactly suited for the gardens of the time – those pleasure grounds which in Germany were little more than sky-ceilinged salons where petty potentates could hold forth to their courtiers, their captive, ever-enthusiastic audience, and generally 'monarchise'.

There are larger rococo gardens of great beauty at the Residenz at Würzburg, now, alas, largely destroyed by bombs, though, miraculously the Tiepolo staircase has survived, and, as we see elsewhere in this book at Schwetzingen near Heidelberg, but nowhere is the spirit of south German rococo more gaily apparent than at Veitshöchheim.

In 1750 the house, for it is far from being a palace, was largely rebuilt and enlarged by the celebrated Balthasar Neumann, the ex-captain of engineers who started his career as a private sol-

A child dressed as a grown-up, on an exquisite rococo plinth carved by Ferdinand Dietz

LEFT: Jockey-capped and garlanded: 'Spring' by the witty and humorous sculptor, Ferdinand Dietz

VEITSHÖCHHEIM

dier, and rose, through his skill as a gun-founder and designer of fountains, to be architect of the Residenz at Würzburg.

All German baroque and rococo gardens owe much, it cannot be denied, to French and Italian examples. But in one form of garden-embellishment a national characteristic was soon to manifest itself: a taste for imaginative and highly decorative sculpture. Of this Veitshöchheim presents the perfect example, and luckily, thanks to careful restoration and repair, its statuary is still there for us to enjoy.

The garden escaped the Romantic wave which swept Germany about 1770, and it owes its survival to the good taste and knowledge of the Prince Bishop of Würzburg of the day, Adam von Seinsheim, and his garden architect, the Bohemian Johann Mayer, who helped him to develop the garden of the Würzburg Residenz. Veitshöchheim had belonged to the Prince Bishops of Würzburg for a hundred and fifty years, and had been for the first eighty years of its history used as a game preserve. What is now the Schloss was a hunting lodge, tucked away unobtrusively in the corner.

Gradually, through the eighteenth century, the game coverts became a garden, and the garden, as it grew, bosquet by bosquet and parterre by parterre, was peopled with statues. The first, commissioned by the Prince Bishop von Greiffenklau, the patron of Tiepolo, were by the sedate chisel of Johann von der Auvera, who conjured several noble figures – an Apollo, a

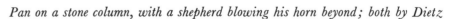

Characterization verging on caricature, by Dietz   *Pan on a stone column, with a shepherd blowing his horn beyond; both by Dietz*

Venus and some muses, which are full of classic calm and solemnity which would not seem out of place at Versailles.

Pegasus, symbol of immortality, the horse we also see sculpted in the gardens at Powerscourt, appears at Veitshöchheim too: it is said that it was from a kick of his hoof that the true Hippocrene, inspiration of poets, first flowed. As on Mount Helicon, at Veitshöchheim, Pegasus also surmounts a fountain where, washed by the water's spray, he caracols against the sky. But his creator was not the solemn Auvera but the greatest of all German baroque sculptors, Ferdinand Dietz, a high spirited and humorous artist who seems himself to embody the very spirit of his age; it is owing to him that a collection of very different sculpture was soon to make its appearance at Veitshöchheim. Rococo at its most sophisticated, a laughing throng of light-hearted statues, impersonating, in stone, pagan deities, the Seasons, or the Continents, with one particularly uproarious figure as Spring, in a flower-decked jockey-cap, and a bedizened negro as America. These are the joyous statues at Veitshöchheim which make the visitor wonder if his eyes see true. Surely he must be imagining things; surely carved stone, which so often depicts emotions such as majesty, sorrow or pride, has never before been utilized to record such human sentiments as these; surely chisel was never used more wittily, or humour more sympathetically been turned to stone? They are remembered long after the other wonders of the gar-

A trophy of the chase

A view from the roof of the Schloss showing the pattern of the garden outlined in its hornbeam hedges

den, the Chinese pavilions, the shell-temple, and the grotto of jewelled serpents and chimeras, have been forgotten.

Of the larger Dietz figures, Nicolas Powell, in his excellent book, *From Baroque to Rococo*, has written:

> It would be hard to decide whether these are to be preferred to the dancing putti dressed as grown-ups, or to his Chinese pavilion in the form of palm trunks supporting a peaked roof with large pine-apples at the corners . . . The garden with its mazes, open-air theatre, thickets and patterns forms the most imaginative complex. With the impertinence and grace of Dietz one is confronted with the very best of late rococo imagination, a last affirmation before the severities of classicism and a new age overwhelmed even southern Germany.

The delights of the gardens of Veitshöchheim are still there for visitors to see, the *pièces d'eau* with their swans and willows, the sculpted palm trees still rearing their trunks, and offering their jumbo-sized pineapples to the surprised Bavarian sky, the cherubs still showing off in their grown-up finery. Overall persists a feeling of fun and gusto and the joy of life; and when we think of Veitshöchheim it is the memory of Dietz's romping figures which lingers, of stone, stained peach or pearl or the colour of pot-pourri by the passing years, highly amused at the idea that anyone should seriously have taken them for gods or goddesses. Great art? Beautiful? As the art critic of *The Times* said in his article on the 1954 Rococo Exhibition, 'It becomes absurd to ask . . . as a technical performance they are overwhelming and it would be ludicrous to look for depth of feeling in anything so extreme, so stylish, so absolutely indifferent to any conceivable criticism that moderation or common sense might apply.'

Weeping willows growing on the brink of the Grosse See

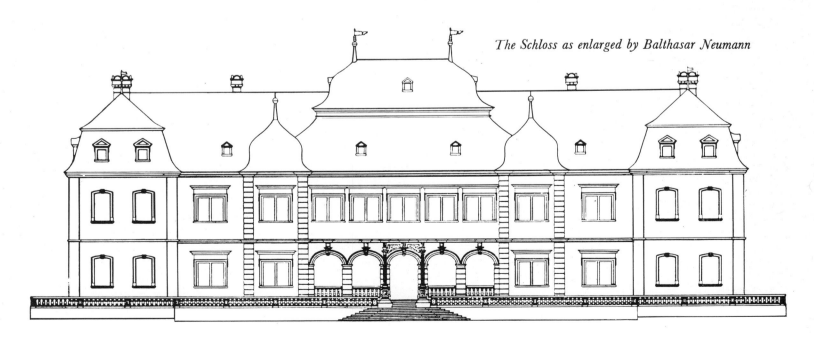

The Schloss as enlarged by Balthasar Neumann

LEFT: *By the 'sedate chisel' of Johann Wolfgang von der Auvera (1724–54), Euterpe, Muse of the Flute, against a background of copper beech*

Cheerful statuary in a rococo garden

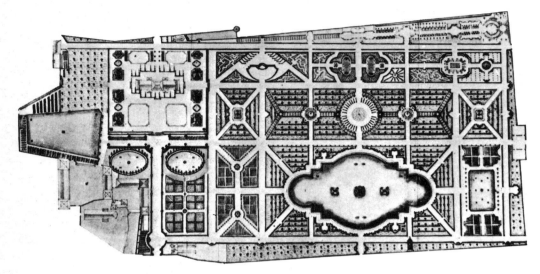

ABOVE: *The elaborate ground plan of the garden at Veitshöchheim*

RIGHT: *A statue of the Muse, Erato, by von der Auvera: the elegantly reconstructed wooden gazebo follows a design of Antonio Petrini*

BELOW: *The gates of the garden silhouetted against the evening sky*

America, feather-girdled and beturbaned, by Dietz

Courances SEINE-ET-OISE

Where water dominates the garden

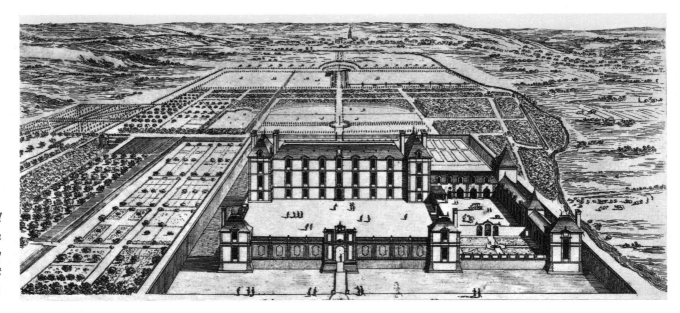

Courances and its park. From an engraving by Israel Henriet (1590–1661)

La Dame de Gallard with the plan of the château and park in 1660. By Beaubrun

La blancheur et le courant des eaux de ce beau lieu l'ont fait nommer Courances.

THE HISTORY OF THE OWNERS OF Courances since the middle Ages reads like a page from Froissart. In the twelfth century it belonged to Guillaume De Milly, in the fourteenth to the Chevalier de Mousseau and later to Raoul du Broc, in the fifteenth to the Seigneur de Marchaumont. The property remained from 1498 to 1622 in the hands of this family until it was sold for 120,000 livres to Claude Gallard, *Conseiller Notaire et Secrétaire* to the King of France. It was his son Claude who built the Château and laid out the gardens almost on the plan we see today, and as they are shown to us by his charming daughter-in-law, Anne Vialart, La Dame de Gallard, in the interesting picture by Beaubrun. Courances remained in the possession of this family, or their female descendants, until the Revolution, when the reigning Seigneur of Courances, Aimard-Charles-Marie de Nicolay, in spite of being an upright and enlightened figure in the last Parliament of Louis XVI, died on the scaffold. After his death Courances fell on evil days. But in 1872 it was bought and largely rebuilt by the great-grandfather of the present owner, the Marquis de Ganay.

The history of the present château and garden of Courances starts about 1622 when they were rebuilt and relaid out on the site of an earlier, moated manor-house. This is described in an

RIGHT: *The moat below the east façade*

COURANCES

Water is the element basic to Courances

A couchant lion by the cascadette

'When one thinks of Courances, one thinks of water . . .'

RIGHT: *The north front*

La Baigneuse, and in the foreground a moss grown dolphin

From an upper window, the great box parterre and mirror pond beyond

The north façade is much as it was when it greeted visitors in the mid seventeenth century

The parterre of box

existing document thus: 'It comprises a lodge with a *pont-levis*, château, towers, *colombier-à-pieds*, terraces, etc., all surrounded by a moat of sweet water. In front of the château is a park, called the small park, with a *basse-cour*. Behind is the large park with kitchen garden, fruit-orchards, canal, parterres, etc.' The whole of what in Scotland would be called 'the policies', for which no exact English word exists, measured forty-eight *arpents* and was enclosed on one side by walls, and on the other by the River Ecole, which ran past and helped to feed the several stretches of ornamental water, the *pièces d'eau* which were always a feature of the place. In the elegant and erudite note on Courances, published in the *Gazette Illustrée Des Amateurs De Jardins*, to which we are indebted for our information about the early history of Courances, the Marquis de Ganay states that the old château was almost certainly built by Claude Gallard in the years following 1622: the chapel, for instance, is dated 1626.

A most interesting engraving of the new Courances exists. It is by Israel Henriet (1590–1661) and shows the façade which greeted visitors in the mid-seventeenth century. In it the *pont levis* has given place to a splendid, almost triumphal, arch, flanked by an elaborately decorated wall and three debonair pavilions. To the right lies a little garden, *un parterre precieux* set with broderies and ornamented with a fountain: over the high tipped roof of the château we see the spreading parterres and bosquets which suggest Versailles.

Since Claude Gallard's rebuilding, the château was altered several times, not always happily. After the Revolution it was abandoned completely for many years: trees grew where now the Ganay family dine; and the gardens, too, suffered complete neglect and dereliction. Today, however, they have been restored much to the plan they followed when first laid out in the seventeenth century. They are without doubt among the most beautiful of the Ile de France.

One trace survives of the gardens of Courances as drawn by Henriet, to the left of whose engraving, among the orchards, can be discerned a small square building, with a dome-shaped roof. This building must have been the centre of the *pièce d'eau* which still exists, and was still called the *dôme* in the eighteenth century. The building itself has gone, but the four shell-shaped fountains which surrounded it are still there, and are said to date from Henry IV. The rest of the garden owes its present perfection to a series of restorations, which have completely revived the classical beauty of plan which La Dame de Gallard exhibits.

The approach to Courances is most impressive, with the symmetry of the ancient walls, and beyond the grille, two *tapis verts* on either side of the central allée, and mirrors of water sumptuously bordered with plane-trees. These present a grave yet poetic picture, ordered and calm, with the splendid regularity of the trees lit from below by the water's play. The majestic plane-trees which are the glory of the approach to Courances were planted in 1782 to take the place of elms.

'Who designed the gardens?' writes the Marquis de Ganay, and goes on to say: 'The name of Le Nôtre has often been mentioned, but there is no proof . . . however tradition has it that the design of the forecourt, at least, is due to him: its air of grandeur and magnificence makes it more than probable.'

The general plan of the gardens of Courances today has changed little since the seventeenth century. There have of course been many changes of detail: the fountains, for which Courances was once celebrated, are no more; but the still mirror-like quality of the *pièces d'eau* with their reflections, give the gardens a compensating calm. The great circular bassin – centre of the axes of the garden – which we see in Henriet's engraving, was replaced in 1750 by the impressive mirror pond which lies framed in the shaven emerald of a lawn, itself richly bordered by the trees which are the beauty of Courances. Beyond, in this century, another bassin was added, and decorated with a sculpted 'Children on a Dolphin'.

The lateral allées shown in Henriet's plan, still lie to right and left, and are now lined with statues. Nearby is a half-moon-shaped *pièce d'eau* over which a nymph, with gushing urn, keeps watch on a lonely pedestal above a flowing spring. This statue is one of great appeal and is the work of Poirier; it came from the gardens of Marly. The late Marquise de Ganay, moving spirit in the restoration of the gardens of Courances, entrusted the work of their recreation to the well known garden architect Achille Duchêne. It was he who also restored two other impressive features of the original garden, the *salle d'eau*, to the east of the château, and the eight fine allées which converged, in the eighteenth century at the 'Gladiator' statue, mentioned by Dezallier d'Argenville in his *Environs de Paris*. This great work of restoration was started before the First World War, and by great fortune was just finished by the fateful month of July 1914.

Madame de Ganay added to the refurbished graces of Courances, a garden of her own, and very much in the taste of her own time: this is the delightful Japanese garden which lies near the eighteenth-century *foulerie*, now a summer-house, and where once grapes were prepared for wine-making. This new garden, with its moss-grown rockwork, is planted informally with ferns, weeping willows (how charmingly they are named in French – *pleureurs*) and many Japanese maples which fill the eye with colour with their burning leaves in spring and again in autumn.

An old rhyme runs:

Les parterres de Cély
Les bois de Fleury
Les eaux de Courances
Sont trois merveilles en France

'*Two tapis verts on either side of the central allée, and mirrors of water . . .*'

The cascadette

And it is true to say that when one thinks of Courances, one thinks of water, the element from which it took its name. For there is water in different forms everywhere at Courances: plangent, falling from the mouths of moss-grown dolphins – 'from each enough to turn a mill', according to Dezallier. Only the restless jet of fountains is missing. Dulaure, another writer of the eighteenth century, stresses the fact that it is water which beautifies and gives life to Courances, 'being an effect of Nature, it flows without stopping – unlike some grandiose cascades which seem with considerable effort to come to life only occasionally, and have to rest afterwards,' – was this an implied criticism of the artificiality of Versailles? – ... 'like a painting which might disappear and leave an empty frame.'

LEFT: *La Baigneuse, by Poirier, which once graced the gardens of Marly*

The Nymphenburg MUNICH
Pavilions and fountains of the Bavarian Court

Schloss Nymphenburg by Canaletto Bernardo Belotto

IN 1654 THE WORTHY but pedestrian Elector Ferdinand Maria of Bavaria married a dashing Italian Princess, Adelaide of Savoy, and his whole life, and the life of Munich his capital, was transformed overnight. Ferdinand, who had succeeded as Elector in 1651, had hitherto devoted his talents, such as they were, to repairing some of the damage done to Bavaria during the Thirty Year War. He had encouraged industry and agriculture, and had already achieved some success. With the arrival of the joyous Princess Adelaide the good work went on, but slowly; much of the money from the Exchequer which had hitherto been used to encourage the ravaged economy of the country was now employed in building palaces and laying out gardens. Balls, masques and routs succeeded each other at Court, and under the sceptre of Electress Adelaide, Munich became one of the most brilliant and light-hearted capitals of Europe. Unfortunately, such was her *train de vie*, that Adelaide seemed to find no time to provide an heir to the throne, and Ferdinand had almost given up hope when, after eight hectic years of marriage, an heir unexpectedly appeared. In high delight, and as a reward, the Elector gave orders that work should at once be started on the new country palace for which his wife had always longed. It was to be called the Nymphaeum, a sanctuary for nymphs, and it was built near Munich by an Italian architect who had come to

RIGHT: *A statue of Mercury before the garden façade*

THE NYMPHENBURG

Bavaria in Princess Adelaide's train, Agostino Barelli. Barelli was succeeded in his work by another Italian, Enrico Zucalli, who was also employed in the work on another Bavarian Palace, Schleissheim, of which the garden plan, with its important central canal, closely resembles that of the Nymphaeum, or 'Nymphenburg', as Adelaide's new pleasure-dome soon came to be called.

Worn out, perhaps, with excitement and new-found frivolity, Elector Ferdinand died in 1679. His son, the Elector Maximilian Emmanuel, was very different to his pleasure-loving parents: bellicose and ambitious, he soon went to war, first with the Turks, and afterwards embroiled his country disastrously with Austria. After the final defeat of Hochstadt in 1704, Bavaria was divided between Austria and the Elector Palatine, and the unlucky Maximilian had to cool off in an eleven-year exile in Paris. While there, however, he had time on his hands to study the latest French style of garden planning.

In 1714 his territories were restored to him, and no sooner had he regained his capital than work began once more on his gar-

The high jet of a fountain leaps towards the clouds

Maria Amalia shot deer from the roof of the Amalienburg

162

The garden façade at Nymphenburg

An airview of the Nymphenburg as it is today

An engraving by M. Wening showing the Nymphenburg in 1701

Orpheus in stone

den at Nymphenburg. He had brought French garden architects back with him, chief among them being François Girard, who completed the palace of Nymphenburg itself, and set about completing the gardens.

As the visitor approaches the Palace from the town, his road skirts a canal, led from the river Würm. This length of water ends before the Palace walls, in two great *piéces d'eau* with important fountains. The line of the canal, main axis of the whole garden, continues on the further garden side of the Palace, and the two water-ways are connected by narrower rivulets which encircle both the Court of Honour, the Palace itself and the parterre which lies garden-wards. These smaller canals join up once more to form the head of the long canal which runs away almost as far as one can see, with green lawns and groves of trees on either side, towards the village of Pasing, whose church tower breaks the sky-line.

Von Rothenstein, a well known traveller, who visited Nymphenburg in 1781 leaves a breathless account of the many fountains and statues which then made the glory of the garden, before the Romantic wave broke over it, and swept away most of its gay decorations:

'The garden has nineteen fountains, which give out 285 jets and such a number of water devices, gilt vases and statues meet the eye, that they are better imagined than described.' Then he goes on to list, in awe, 'Six gilt urns, $3\frac{1}{2}$ ells in height . . . dragon fountains to right and left, with many dragons and snakes lying on separate hills of stone . . . children seated on gilt whales . . . a zephyr, astonished by a monkey with a basket . . . a gilt lion – a shaggy dog – three large swans, two storks, and a great deal of sea-weed' (in what medium, one wonders?) 'as well as Tritons with their hands full of pearls and coral.' Such, in 1781, were the wonders of the garden at Nymphenburg. Most have gone, and the garden today, though grandiose in conception and extent is far simpler and less spectacular. But three exquisite pavilions, mercifully, have survived from the original plan, and still make a visit to Nymphenburg memorable.

These are the *Maisons de Plaisance*, built by Maximilian and his successor Charles Albert, which regularly dot the garden, or rather, as it is today, the park. They recall the garden houses at Peterhof built by Le Blond for Peter the Great: Marly and Mon Plaisir. The first, built in 1716 as a garden 'green-room' for actors and actresses in the outdoor theatre to dress and rest in, was built in the oriental style and called Pagodenburg. It makes an enchanting picture, nestling among the high park trees; its interior resembles the *Trianon de Porcelaine* at Versailles, of which Max Emmanuel may well have heard tales when in exile in France. The Saletl or little salon of the Pagodenburg shimmers in blue and white tiles and the oriental atmosphere is heightened as the visitor gains the Chinese room where he finds walls of coromandel and a ceiling of chinoiserie. The Pagodenburg was built for Maximilian Emmanuel by the talented Bavarian Josef Effner, as was the nearby Badenburg, in 1718. This is simpler; with its pearly stucco decoration and inviting Delft tiled swimming pool.

But it is the Amalienburg, the third and most famous pavilion in the garden at Nymphenburg which has been hailed as the one 'immortal creation of Bavarian rococo'. It was built in 1734 as a hunting box for Maria Amalia of Austria, wife of the Elector Karl Albrecht, who used to shoot driven deer from the gilded grill on its roof, a perfect picture for a tapestry. Its architect was François Cuvilliés, who was born at Soignies in 1695, and began life as a Court dwarf. The Elector, then in exile, noticed his talents and brought him to study architecture in Paris under François Blondel. It was this Frenchman, ill-formed, but with innate good taste who, according to Henry Channon, that lover of Bavaria and the rococo, 'splashed Munich with his gracious genius'.

One enters the Amalienburg through the gun-room (was it not a hunting box?) panelled in blue and white Delft china, with dog kennels below the gun-cupboards; passing through the Elector's closet, with faded brocade to hide the *chaise percée*, one gains a chamber 'elaborate with silver carvings foaming over ochre walls', and a singularly un-inviting alcove bed. Finally there is 'the octagonal hall of mirrors which is the soul of the building – the paragon of the whole eighteenth century' and Henry Channon goes on to record:

> Against a pale grey blue background, a confusion of cool silver . . . fiddlers and harps, flowing jugs and banners, garlands and festoons, emblems of the chase, stags, nets and fish . . . nymphs brandishing symbols of country pursuits . . . on the ceiling and flying low, are pigeons, duck, snipe, a silver hoopoe. There is a cascade's coolness, and over them all a silver glow lends a veil of light so that there is a feeling of blue infinity of silver lace spread over a transparent sea, spray splashing on water, crystals glistening among aquamarines.

This, then, is the Amalienburg, which weaves the same spell as do the Dietz statues at Veitshöchheim. It has come, for the author of this book at least, to enshrine the very essence of Nymphenburg. All the pavilions lose much, of course, by being shorn of their original elaborate setting; and in fact, in the original garden plan they played a far more important part, architecturally, than they do today. Skell, whose work we see at Schwetzingen, where he showed laudable restraint, laid a harder hand on the Nymphenburg, sweeping away most of the conceits which had so taken Von Rothenstein's eye in 1781. No longer do the pavilions, in frameworks of fountains and flower garden, dominate the cross axes of the garden: the trees have grown and the *parterres precieuses* have disappeared: but miraculously the pavilions themselves still exist. Leave the warm park and enter their iridescent rooms, and you will feel the full magic of the rococo.

Shell and pebblework walls in the Magdalenenklause built in 1728

Distant view of the house from the great fountain

Bagatelle NEAR PARIS
The fairest rose-garden in France

The north façade of the pavilion

Si vous voulez vous promener
Dans ce Bois, charmante Isabelle,
Nous pourrons, sans nous détourner,
Aller jusqu'à Bagatelle.

THE STORY OF BAGATELLE has been often told, but it is so fascinating that no description of the garden would be complete without an idea, at least, of the history of the place.

In 1777 the young and frivolous brother of Louis XVI, the Comte d'Artois, wanting to surprise and please his sister-in-law Marie Antoinette, with whom, it was said, he was a little in love, offered to build a palace for her in two months. The Queen was flattered and delighted, but laid a wager of 100,000 livres that such a thing was impossible. The Court was just leaving Versailles for its autumn visit to Fontainebleau. D'Artois took the bet, and promised that the new palace and its gardens would be ready for the Queen when she returned to Versailles sixty days later.

They were, but at immense cost and by using methods which were widely criticized. The Austrian Ambassador, always slightly disapproving of the Queen and her entourage, was scandalized, as can be seen from a letter he wrote to Marie Antoinette's mother, the Empress Maria Theresa:

> A few days before the departure to Fontainebleau, M. Le Comte d'Artois had the idea of demolishing a little house he has in the Bois de Boulogne, called Bagatelle, and rebuilding it entirely . . . and to give a fête for the Queen there when the Court returns to Versailles. At first it appeared an impossible feat to do in seven weeks, but, with the aid of nine hundred workmen of every kind, working day and night, it has been done . . . What is unheard of is the way the work was carried out.

The shocked Ambassador goes on to describe how the Comte's Swiss guards requisitioned any carts carrying building materials such as lime or stone which they could find on the high roads round Paris, whoever they belonged to: they were paid for, apparently, but many people were incensed and inconvenienced by the Comte's high-handed action.

RIGHT: *Pillars of roses make the splendour of the garden in June*

BAGATELLE

The lake

To urge on the work, d'Artois seldom left the scene of activities, supervising the plans and generally interfering and getting in the way. To keep the workmen in a good temper, barrels of wine were constantly on tap, and as the building had to go on day and night, while the white palace quickly rose, stone by stone, by the light of torches, the work was enlivened by musicians who were constantly in attendance, playing bagpipes and barrel-organs.

Work had started on 22nd September. The workmen and gardeners were under the direction of the Comte's architect, Alexandre Bélanger, and his Scottish gardener Blaikie, and the palace and garden were, incredible as it seems, completed exactly sixty-four days later. The Queen lost her bet, but was enchanted, the Comte triumphant, although his exploit had cost him 3,000,000 livres, or, in today's currency, nearly a quarter of a million pounds ($700,000).

The Pavilion of Bagatelle, small, white and exquisite, with its windows garlanded in carved roses and its door flanked with sphinxes with their faces and bosoms modelled from those of one of the Comte d'Artois' mistresses, the actress Rosalie Duthé, looks today much as it did when it was first built; but the gardens, among the most beautiful in France, have undergone many changes.

In 1777, anything English was fashionable in France. English horse-racing, English clothes, and now, suddenly, English gardens. The romantic movement and the return to nature were at their height across the Channel, and the new English ideas had been put into practice by a great friend of the Comte d'Artois, Comte de Chimay. The Queen had admired the garden he had newly laid out in the English style, and the Comte decided that his new pleasure ground, Bagatelle, should follow the same fashionable trend. Blaikie had a staff of over forty to assist him in his task, which was not an easy one, as the soil was poor and stony. Before any planting could be done tons of earth had to be carted to the site.

Near the Pavilion itself, and quite in keeping, Blaikie laid out a formal garden which has a distant view of the fortress of Mont Valérien. Further away he allowed his gift for the new form of gardening to have full scope; here, following the precepts of Capability Brown, who got his nickname not because of his undoubted efficiency but because he always spoke of studying the 'Capabilities' of the site, Blaikie conjured slopes where everything was level, and laid serpentine paths which led through romantic thickets to mossy arbours and grottoes. He was a master of his art, and for a Scotsman, full of fantasy. As well as a *jardin français* he devised a real *jardin chinois*, with a stream and pagoda, to bring to mind the pattern of willow-pattern china.

In 1789 the Revolution put an end to the brief but gay reign of the Comte d'Artois at Bagatelle. Three months after the fall of the Bastille he went into exile, and was not to see his enchanting domain for twenty-four years. The Revolution spared the Pavilion of Bagatelle itself, although its contents were carried away and auctioned. There was a move to tear the house down, but fortunately it was prevented, although the neighbouring Château de Madrid was destroyed. The National Assembly took possession of Bagatelle, which it was decided, should be *affectué aux Réjouissances Populaires*. In fact, it seems that the Commune of Neuilly, in which Bagatelle was located, went to some pains to preserve the amenities of their newly acquired pleasure-ground. For on the 28 May 1794, in the last days of the Terror, they invited *tous les citoyens et citoyennes se promenant à Bagatelle, à ne toucher à rien, à s'y comporter avec décence, à peine d'être arrêté et conduit devant les autorités constituées.*

However, in 1797, the domain was split up, and was leased to various *restaurateurs* and tradespeople, who organized the property on the lines of the Vauxhall gardens in London. The pavilion became a fashionable restaurant and the park a popular place of resort for Parisians who were entertained there by bands, dancing and balloon ascents, and by gazing at the beauties of the Directoire, the *Merveilleuses*, among them Madame Tallien and Joséphine de Beauharnais, who promenaded under the Japanese lanterns which were hung among the trees.

Under the Empire, Bagatelle was bought back by the Crown and Napoleon refurnished it and used it as a hunting box. The gardens were restored, and the King of Rome, Napoleon's son by his second Empress, Marie Louise, would come and play in them. Sometimes Joséphine, divorced for her inability to provide the Emperor with an heir, would visit the gardens once more to see him playing there. At the Restoration Bagatelle again changed hands, and the Comte d'Artois, older and more sober, retook possession, making few changes except to remove some of the more daring wall-paintings, relics of his free and easy youth.

It was under the Second Empire that Bagatelle blossomed anew. It was bought in 1835 by the enormously rich Marquess of Hertford. By the time Napoleon III succeeded, the estate and garden had been greatly increased and developed. Additions had been made to the house, and many of Blaikie's charming garden contrivances were swept away. The Chinese temples and romantic grottoes had disappeared, to be replaced with *volières* and belvederes. The Park had been doubled in size, and a riding school, on the site of the present rose garden, laid out. Many statues, some from Vaux and Versailles, had been set up in the garden. These were Lord Hertford's special pride, and there is a story that when two of his friends asked to be allowed to settle an affair of honour by fighting a duel in the grounds of Bagatelle, Lord Hertford forbade it; not, as he said, out of any interest in the fate of either of his friends, but for fear that their pistol shots might damage his statues.

Bagatelle, throughout the Second Empire, was a great centre

The Comte d'Artois, afterwards Charles X (1757–1836) and the Empress Eugénie (1826–1920)

The Kiosque de l'Impératrice in the rose-garden

of entertaining, with the Emperor and Empress constant guests. The Prince Imperial often used to ride there, and the Empress would watch him from the little kiosque, which still overlooks what is now the rose garden. Eugénie, in fact, received the news of the outbreak of war with Prussia while at Bagatelle, at a children's party in the garden for her son.

With the fall of the Empire and the death of Lord Hertford in 1870 another chapter opened in the history of Bagatelle. It was inherited by Sir Richard Wallace, Lord Hertford's natural son, who removed the house's magnificent contents to London (now the Wallace Collection), for fear of them being damaged in the excesses of the Commune.

Sir Richard lived at Bagatelle for many years in princely style, adding to the house, not very happily, and building the adjacent Trianon, designed by Léon de Sauges, to provide extra space. Twenty gardeners kept the gardens trim. On Sir Richard Wallace's death the property passed to his widow, who in turn left it to her secretary, Sir John Murray Scott.

Robert Joffet, devoted Honorary *Conservateur en Chef* of the gardens of Paris, has described the sale, which now took place, of the property of Bagatelle to the City of Paris:

'At the beginning of the Century, the rumour circulated that the Park of Bagatelle was to be split up. Paris was shocked: and on the suggestion of my predecessor J. C. N. Forestier, the Municipality of Paris, following a decision taken on 25th March 1904, authorised the expropriation of the property and its incorporation into the Bois de Boulogne.' The price was about 6½ million francs, and in January 1905 the sale was completed.

Forestier, a most distinguished gardener and plant-lover, drew up his proposals for putting the property of Bagatelle to fullest use and for the most complete enjoyment of the people of Paris, its new owners.

The gist of his report ran thus:

Bagatelle, quite apart from its situation in the Bois de Boulogne, is unique historically and on account of the memories it evokes. By restoring it and planting it afresh, we could assemble there collections of flowers, which are best suited for gardens, not only plants that are of possibly scientific and botanical interest: for instance, trees, shrubs and ornamental plants. There would be a rose-garden, a collection of rock-plants, a collection of hardy plants which have gone out of fashion, climbers, heaths, lilacs and so on. England has Kew Gardens – which in no sense would we copy – but they might well be our inspiration.

The benefits to French horticulture and domestic garden art which such an enterprise would bring would justify every effort. Nurserymen and plant collectors would surely help us, and thus the garden of Bagatelle would be preserved, not only as a fascinating survival from the Eighteenth Century, but a living example of garden evolution.

The suggestions of Forestier were faithfully followed, and twenty-four hectares of garden were gradually developed.

A French wallpaper of 1800 in the Metropolitan Museum 'Les Jardins de Bagatelle'

LEFT: *The rose-garden, looking towards the orangery*

The Comte d'Artois flanked the entrance to the pavilion with sphinxes modelled on his mistress

The gardens today comprise some of the early features such as the Comte d'Artois' rockwork and lake, his artificial ruins, and of course his trees, now grown to their full maturity. Of Lord Hertford's additions we see the French garden, the water-lily lake, with the lotus and rare water plants and his lake of black swans. Forestier planned a charming garden of iris, where today a memorial tablet has been placed in his honour. But it is the rose garden at Bagatelle, planned and planted by Quentin Bauchart in 1906, which is the chief glory of Bagatelle today. It fills the paddock where the Prince Imperial used to ride, and on one side, on a little rise, with a background of fine oaks, the *Kiosque de l'Imperatrice* still overlooks the sun-lit, flower-filled scene. The rose garden is not, like the celebrated Roseraie de l'Hay, nearby, an exhaustive collection of every rose that exists, but it is planted with roses that are purely decorative: roses, in fact, for every garden, and in May and June the gardens present a wonderful picture – with parasols of rose-trees loaded with flowers, climbing roses grown in obelisks which are literally pillars of pink, white or crimson, and brimming beds, outlined in shaven box, of Hybrid Tea roses laying their heady scent on the air around.

Since 1907 an International Competition of New Roses has been held at Bagatelle, where all year round, the growing habits, relative strengths, flowering periods and so on of new roses are closely studied and tabulated. At the annual Competition, an international jury judges the flowers and awards the prizes; and the wide interest taken in the winning roses insures their distribution to gardens throughout France and in other countries, thus raising the standard of rose-growing everywhere.

Bagatelle offers examples of many styles of gardening, but the whole concept has a certain unity. Flower-colour has been used, but the modern flower beds, while delighting the eye with their brightness, have not been allowed to impinge on their classical setting. Their colours have been used to underline and accentuate, not to distract from the overall plan. Monsieur Joffet has written of Bagatelle: 'Its owners, have, since the eighteenth century, had a love of nature, gardens and flowers, as well as a taste for elegance . . . In the eighteenth century, particularly, charming though doubtless frivolous women have held sway at Bagatelle: their wit was surely quick and light, their conversation sparkling, their manners distinguished. Above all, they were adepts at the art of pleasing.'

Today, the park of Bagatelle attracts hundreds of thousands of visitors, mainly women, who seem specially attracted by the charm of Bagatelle.

Promettez-moi de m'avertir
Toutes les fois, chère Isabelle,
Que vous aurez quelque désir
De faire un tour à Bagatelle.

Cuddling cupids over the shell fountain

Marlia NEAR LUCCA

Where concerts were given in an open-air theatre

Pantaloon strikes an attitude in the Teatro di Verdura

ONE SUMMER EVENING, SAY IN 1812, while at the other side of Europe Napoleon was preparing for his invasion of Russia, a highly civilized scene might have been witnessed in the garden of a villa in Tuscany. A group of men and women, elegantly dressed in the height of Empire fashion, the men knee-breeched and silk-stockinged, the women in high-waisted dresses of rich silk, their short hair dressed in the antique style and their faces and necks framed in the *cherusque*, the high Vandyke style of collar made fashionable by the Empress Joséphine, would be listening to a violin concert in a *Teatro di Verdura*, an open-air theatre, cut from hedges of clipped yew: the violinist would be the most famous of his day – Paganini; the hostess, a handsome, mannish-looking woman, with an opinionated jaw, the Grand Duchess of Tuscany, formerly Madame Baciocchi, formerly Signorina Elisa Buonaparte of Ajaccio. Elisa Baciocchi was a masterful ruler who administered her Grand-Duchy with Napoleonic efficiency: but one of her more human characteristics was her love of music. She married her undistinguished husband because of his gifts as a violinist, and she adored Paganini, who recorded in his memoirs that she sometimes fainted from emotion when he played to her.

Elisa bought the Villa Marlia, driving a hard bargain, as she always did, in 1806, having looked at many other villas round Lucca in her search for what she considered would make a worthy country palace. The villa was one of the finest in the neighbourhood; its gardens were already famous, and the property had a long and distinguished history.

The Villa Reale di Marlia lies north-east of Lucca in Tuscany, at the foot of the Pizzorne hills, a range of the Central Apennines, from which the River Serchio flows to the Mediterranean near Viareggio. The name probably derives from Marilla, or 'small sea', on account of the frequent floods which used to occur in the Serchio area. Though there was a castle on the site from the earliest times, the present villa was built by the noble family of Orsetti about 1651, who also built the graceful Palazzina dell' Orologio with its clock tower, which

RIGHT: *Pebblework paving and piers of rustic flints give access to the Teatro di Verdura*

A giant figure fills the pool with water from an urn

Harlequinade figures stand about in expectant attitudes

flanks it: they also planted the *Teatro di Verdura* which is still such a fascinating feature of the garden.

It is not known who were their architects and designers, though it has been suggested that the celebrated Filippo Juvara (1676–1736), the architect of the fantastic Stupinigi palace in Turin, may have had a hand in laying out the gardens. Certainly, in 1714, Juvara is known to have been engaged in many projects in the Lucca area, and it is quite likely that Stefano Orsetti, celebrated as a *magnifico signore*, would have eagerly sought the services of such a successful and fashionable architect. For Stefano, it appears, suffered from slight *folie de grandeur*, and is said to have changed the name of his property from Marilla to Marlia to underline its likeness to Louis XIV's famous palace at Marly, with which he liked to compare it.

The outstanding feature, besides the theatre, of the gardens at Marlia as they survive today, is the framework of high hedges of ilex and laurel in which the garden is set. In front of the villa lies a wide expanse of lawn, once a paved or pebbled courtyard, and possibly used as a *Manège*, as can be seen in an old engraving. Behind the villa, and opposite the entrance, is a monumental fountain, characteristic of the seventeenth century, in the form of a rocky semicircle, with a gushing cascade, and tufted with moss and ferns, the whole being surmounted with statues of Jupiter, Saturn, Adonis and Pomona. This grandiose concept is backed with architecturally-cut hedges of ilex.

Looking from the fountain to the house, the oldest part of the garden lies to our left. Here, through high piered gates, we enter the Lemon Garden, the *Giardino dei Limoni*. Ahead lies a great basin, a rectangular garden pool, balustraded all round in

176

RIGHT: '*A high twin-pedimented Frontone . . . with a centre niche for a statue of Leda . . .*'

'*Vases . . . brim over with blue plumbago, an unusual and very beautiful combination . . .*'

J. S. Sargent's water-colour of the Lemon Garden

marble, which is dappled with lichen and decorated with terra-cotta vases of lemon trees and flowers. It is these vases and the flowers they contain that show that Marlia is no museum garden, but a place that is loved, where the planting is personally supervised. In any other garden in Italy such vases would almost certainly be filled with geraniums; here they brim over with blue plumbago, an unusual and very beautiful combination, with the colour of the stonework all about. At the head of the pool recline guardian giants in stone, representing the rivers Serchio and Arno, the two great rivers of Tuscany: as a background to these two figures there is a high twin pedimented *Frontone*, an architectural conceit in rusticated stone and pebble work, with a centre niche for a statue of Leda and the Swan.

At the opposite end of the Lemon Garden, and at the far end of a path bordered by bougainvillea trees in pots and more lemons, is another *Frontone*, pebble decorated and bearing the Orsetti coat of arms in the centre; above stand busts of Roman Emperors, and below lies a mermaid-haunted pool.

This Lemon Garden at Marlia was a favourite subject for the famous American artist J. S. Sargent who painted two water-colours of it in the nineties. These water-colours were in the Boston Museum of Fine Arts, but are at the moment in the White House, where they have been lent to Mrs Kennedy, as a souvenir of Marlia, which she visited some years ago. Beyond the Lemon Garden lies the famous theatre, approached through a foyer of tall shorn ilex, with a high-flung fountain, and two seventeenth-century statues of mythological women.

The theatre, planted about 1652, is cut from yew trees, and forms a circular out-door room, with wings, *loges*, conductor's platform, prompter's box, even candleshades cut from the living green. It is one of the most complete 'green theatres' in the world, and like the one at Collodi, certainly one of the few original ones. The stage is of close-cropped grass, and figures of Columbine, Pulcinella and Pantaloon stand about in expectant attitudes, as if the Harlequinade is about to start. All through the eighteenth century, and during Elisa's short reign at Marlia, the theatre was used for amateur theatricals and concerts by the nobility of Lucca.

Elisa first occupied Marlia in 1806 but, having grand ideas, soon found the property too small, and dispossessed her next door neighbour, the Bishop of Lucca, and took over his house, the Vescovato, still part of the Marlia estate. Furthermore, she bought up, at her own prices, as many adjacent properties as she could. Then, and it could have been disastrous had her reign been longer, she started to remodel the garden. For this she called in Morel, who had had a hand in the laying out of the garden at Malmaison for Elisa's sister-in-law Joséphine. Morel proposed to sweep away the old garden entirely, replacing it with a *Parco all' Inglese*, which at that time, in spite of the war, was as much the fashion in France as it was all over the Continent. The formal gardens of the Vescovato disappeared, only a pebble-lined Grotto of Pan being spared, and were replaced with a lake and plantations of trees. Fortunately there was no time to set about the destruction of the theatre, though plans existed for its elimination, nor for sweeping away the high ilex hedges which are the glory of the garden at Marlia.

Elisa also altered the villa radically, and called Theodore Bienaimé from Paris to assist her. The exterior was changed – the ground floor fenestration being enlarged with French windows, the top floor heightened and the graceful belvedere removed. In these notes, in which we are concerned mainly with the garden, there is no room to enumerate the changes indoors: suffice it to say that the old eighteenth-century interior was completely remodelled on Empire lines, by no means unsuccessfully.

The graceful Palazzina dell' Orologio, built about 1651, which greets visitors to Marlia

Below the Vescovato lies a little formal garden of coloured gravel and silver-leafed borders

Two things certainly must be said in favour of Elisa's operations at Marlia: she revived the Carrara marble quarries, and to help this industry ordered quantities of sculpture and especially urns, which she placed in the park and round the house. Many of Bienaimé's sculptures were later bought by the sixth Duke of Devonshire and now adorn the park and avenues at Chatsworth. Elisa also imported many rare trees and exotic shrubs never before grown in Tuscany, which still grow in the garden. However, in 1814, the all-powerful brother, Napoleon, fell, and Elisa, Grand Duchess no longer, retired to obscurity in Trieste.

After Elisa's departure, the domain of Marlia reverted to the Dukes of Parma, then to the Royal Family of Italy. Since then it has been known as the Villa Reale di Marlia: it was fortunate in being bought by Count and Countess Pecci-Blunt in 1923 from local speculators who had acquired it from the heir of the Prince of Capua to whom the King of Italy had made it over.

The gardens have been splendidly maintained. As the original layout of the Vescovato garden had utterly disappeared, it was considered best, in that part of the garden, at least, to carry out Elisa Baciocchi's plan for an English park. Today round the lake are some of the finest and rarest trees of Italy. Count and Countess Pecci-Blunt also planted the great hedges on either side of the lawn, with their statues in recessed niches alternating with borders of flowers. The theatre is meticulously kept, as is the Lemon Garden. Further from the house new gardens have been planted, designed by the well-known French architect Jacques Greber, who laid out the Spanish garden behind the ancient Grotto of Pan, and this garden, with its pools and brimming borders of flowers is full of brilliant colour in autumn, tactfully out of sight of the more classic parts of the garden, like the theatre and the Lemon Garden, where bright colours and herbaceous borders would be quite out of place. Jacques Greber also designed the swimming pool, the twentieth-century equivalent of the eighteenth-century *pièce d'eau*, which was the first in Italy.

For many weeks every summer Count and Countess Pecci-Blunt fill their house with friends from all over the world, offering hospitality which is eighteenth century in its lavishness and charm. The gardens act as extra salons for their happy entertainments. They are memorable, because probably nowhere in the world are there seventeenth-century gardens, privately owned, which are so perfectly preserved; and not only preserved, but exquisitely kept, and further developed every year. One quality, the gardens at Marlia lack – that feeling of nostalgic sadness and dissolution which haunts so many gardens in Italy. There is nothing of that at Marlia; rather they have the radiance of gardens which are loved, and are therefore very much alive.

A great basin, balustraded in marble, which is dappled with lichen

Charleston

Three gardens in a near-tropical setting

A portrait by Benjamin West (1738–1820) of Arthur Middleton, his wife Mary Izzard and his son Henry who became Governor of South Carolina

SOME MILES INLAND FROM CHARLESTON, one of the most historic and loveliest of all the cities of the Southern United States lies an area known as the Low Country, where the climate is benign, and winters are kind. The countryside is watered by two rivers, the Ashley and the Cooper. Water in fact plays a great part in establishing the character and curious charm of the Low Country, with its numerous swamps and slow-gliding rivers. A hundred and fifty years ago rice was the main crop grown, and it thrived astonishingly on the marshy flats in the long hot summers. Today the same succulent black soil on which the rice grew so well provides a rich diet for the spectacular groves of magnolias, camellias and azaleas which make the gardens of Charleston a place of pilgrimage for thousands of Americans.

Three of these Southern gardens are justly celebrated, Middleton, Magnolia and Cypress: of the trilogy, the first, in age is Middleton, which lies on a bend of the Ashley River: its long life story is chequered with light and shade alternating through the centuries: it could be said to have had a prolonged and happy youth, a middle age punctuated with disasters, and a happy old age, with complete rehabilitation to beauty.

MIDDLETON PLACE

Middleton was planned and created by Henry Middleton, Governor of South Carolina, a great American patriot and President of the first Continental Congress. It is the first garden in America to have been landscaped, for as early as 1741 when the terraces and canals of Versailles, that model of all grand gardens, were but sixty years old, a hundred black slaves were clearing vistas at Middleton towards the surrounding savannahs, digging terraces and walks and delving artificial lakes. The work took nine years to complete. Though the garden owes much to French inspiration, the plan of the house itself, now no more, with its central block and spreading wings ending in smaller blocks, recalls many large English country-houses of the

RIGHT: *Waving veils of Spanish moss (Tillandsia usneoides) are a feature of most Southern gardens*

Framed in groups of yuccas, the wide lawns of Middleton Place stretch towards the Ashley river

White azaleas grow down to the water's brink

spacious Georgian age. Only one of the smaller blocks has been restored, but it is easy to trace the site of the original house, which stood on a lengthy terrace on the axis of the main avenue towards the east. On the west lies the great formal lay-out.

Henry Middleton's son Arthur continued to develop and plant his father's garden. He was one of the signers of the Declaration of Independence. Both he and his father had been fervent supporters of the rebellion from its inception, and it is fitting that the terms of surrender for King George's troops and the conditions for their withdrawal from South Carolina should have been signed at Middleton Place; but not before the house, which was a well known centre of anti-British feeling, had been looted by loyalist forces, and much of the gardens damaged. In the peaceful days that followed the revolution, Henry's grandson planted many thousands of camellias. He was a friend of the French botanist André Michaux (for whom the white belled herbaceous plant *Michauxia campanuloides* is named), and it was Michaux who brought the first camellia trees to America in 1783 and planted them at Middleton. Three of the four original trees are still shown to visitors, and flower regularly every year. His son William Middleton, who inherited the gardens in 1846, set some of the first *Azalea indica* to be grown in America, the very first being grown at nearby Magnolia.

This halcyon period, with the azaleas, magnolias and camel-

Peaceful reflections in the rice-mill pond

lias tended by an army of slaves, and growing quickly to perfection under the southern sky, their colours brilliant against the gentle grey melancholy of the surrounding savannahs, was not to last long. Middleton suffered cruelly in the Civil War; and in February 1865, almost at the end of the fighting, a Northern raiding party looted and burnt the house to the ground. Only the southern block remained in a state which allowed restoration; later, in 1886, the ruins were further shaken by an earthquake. But the gardens, or rather much of the original garden plan, and many of the plants, survived.

The present occupant of Middleton Place, Mr Pringle Smith, who is a direct descendant in the female line from the first owner of Middleton, has worked since 1916 to restore the gardens, with the dedicated help of his wife until her death in 1957. The gardens have been enlarged – a nearby hillside has been planted with thousands of azaleas and a cypress lake as well as a new camellia garden created.

The main axis of the garden at Middleton Place is formed by the long site of the great house, of which only the south block remains, running north and south. This lies at right angles to the main avenue which runs east and west. In front of where the house once stood lies the most imposing area of the garden, a gentle hillside sculpted by Henry Middleton's hundred slaves into a series of six graceful grass terraces. Below these lie twin

Hoary tree-trunks by the waterside

The Middleton oak was an Indian 'trail tree' long before Columbus, and has a circumference of 37 feet

lakes designed in the form of a butterfly, its body formed by a causeway of closely shaven turf, and its wings by the water on either side. Beyond lies the shining scimitar of the Ashley River, and beyond that again the monochrome distances of the savannah.

To the south lies the old rice mill, which was driven by tide water from the river and dates from pre-revolutionary days. This stands on the banks of a larger lake which has its brim planted deep with azaleas and flowering shrubs. At one point the lake is spanned by a sophisticated bridge in chinoiserie. Nearby lies a 'moonlight' garden which is uniquely charming and original, for it is planted only with white flowers, and especially those that are strongly scented at night, such as jasmine, gardenias and narcissus.

To the north of the site of the old house the visitor walks through tunnels of camellias, on paths carpeted inches deep in coral from fallen petals. Nearby are Michaux's veteran camellias, America's first, which still begin to bloom each January and are a magnificent sight at their peak towards the middle of February. One tree has a stem five feet in circumference and another is at least thirty feet tall.

Middleton Place offers a supreme example of how a great garden created two centuries ago has grown to mellow maturity. Its plan fits to perfection the lie of the land around, hugging the gentle rise of ground, and melting into the watery landscape. When its flowers are at their fullest beauty in April, May and June, the gardens are visited by tens of thousands of visitors. Their gratitude is due to the past generations of the Middleton family and especially to their descendants for creating, and devotedly maintaining, a garden in America as fine as any that you could find in Europe.

RIGHT: *Spanish moss curtains a view towards the old pre-revolutionary rice-mill*

MAGNOLIA GARDENS

In the Baedeker guide for America in 1900 there are only three sights which were considered worthy of two stars – the Niagara Falls, the Grand Canyon and Magnolia Gardens. Thus, Magnolia was famous over sixty years ago, and even then it was not a newly planted garden, having been created in the 1830's when Andrew Jackson was President. It took its name from a great avenue of magnolias, which years ago led up to the house from the landing stage on the Ashley River. Today only one of these original magnolias survives, an enormous tree with the polished dark-green leaves backed with the brown suede of all the *Magnolia grandiflora* group, and covered in summer with scent-laden white goblets of flowers.

Magnolia Gardens were designed by the Reverend John Grimke Drayton whose ancestors had long lived in Carolina, having come there by way of Barbados in the seventeenth century. He took to gardening for reasons of health, as his doctor told him that his ministerial duties kept him too much indoors. There were already magnificent natural features on the site, of which the Reverend John took full advantage. One of the indigenous trees of Carolina which grows to perfection at Magnolia is the Swamp Cypress, and these the garden creator used as a background for some of his most dramatic plantings, setting banks of flaming azaleas against the trees' dark cloisteral stems, to reflect their brilliant colour in the water all about. The Swamp Cypress, *Taxodium distichum*, is a tree dating from the earliest days of the evolution of our vegetation. Though there are fine examples in Europe, at Kew and in the park at Versailles near Marie Antoinette's 'hameau', its home is the southern coast of America where trees are found of immense age and height. The roots of the Swamp Cypress exude tannic acid, which stains the water around them inky black: this dramatises reflections still more, and gives the gardens of South Carolina a unique pictorial quality. Taxodiums have yet another peculiarity. Their roots send up 'knees', hollow, woody protuberances which form round the cypress's base, and add to their odd and striking appearance as they rise tall and straight out of the ebony water.

Another natural feature that the Reverend John found were groves of Live Oaks, *Quercus virginiana*: these, too, grow in South Carolina to enormous size. Evergreen, and akin to the English ilex, beloved of Disraeli for its aristocratic appearance, the Live Oaks of Magnolia are often host to what is perhaps the most characteristic of all southern vegetation, the strange Spanish moss, *Tillandsia usneoides*, which shrouds their stems and boughs with eerie drifting veils of grey, and at once creates everyone's idea of a garden of the South.

Against the background of these splendid trees, by the sable-

Magnolia soulangeana

LEFT: *Sculptured lawns by the lakeside in the garden of Middleton Place*

Spanish moss drapes overhanging branches

hued waters of the lake, the creator of Magnolia Gardens plant-
ed in 1848 the first *Azalea indica* ever to be grown in America.
Their descendants flower there today, and probably more beau-
tifully and generously than anywhere else in the world, for at
Kew there is a notice near the azalea plantations which reads,
'Azaleas in their highest glory are to be found in Magnolia
Gardens, near Charleston, South Carolina, U.S.A.'

Besides azaleas and magnolias there are magnificent plantings of camellias of every variety, many of which were raised
in the highly successful nursery which the present owner of
Magnolia runs nearby. But the flowers and shrubs of Magnolia
are innumerable, and as the visitor walks through its glades, his
eye is caught and continually entranced, whether it is by a
Cherokee Rose, that lovely snowy golden-centered American
flower, *Rosa laevigata,* wreathing its way towards the sky through
a tall tree's branches, or by a giant banksian rose falling in a
shower of gold over a Hackberry tree, *Celtis occidentalis.*

The present owner of Magnolia, Mr C. Norwood Hastie, is a
direct descendant of the Reverend John Grimke Drayton, and
works hard to keep the gardens at their highest pitch of beauty.
He warmly welcomes the visitors who in their thousands drive
the fifteen miles from Charleston every spring to visit the gardens. As they wander through their flower-filled walks, over the
scented air they hear the clear call of the mocking bird and the
never ceasing drone of frogs. Memory stirs in the slowly moving
veils of Spanish moss; in a grove of oaks by the river's path they
come on a marble tomb. Carved on it are these words: 'Reverend John Grimke Drayton 1815–91. Creator of this garden,
the spirit of which speaks more eloquently than words of the
vision which was his.'

A crisply painted white bridge finds its twin in the water below

White azaleas mirrored by the waterside

CYPRESS GARDENS

One of the unforgettable memories of a lifetime is passing through the canals of Venice in a gondola. A visit to the Cypress Gardens, third in the trilogy of great Charleston gardens, makes a similar impression; for the gardens can be visited by boat, and as one glides silently through the flower-walled channels, over the ink-black water, bright with flower reflections, even the colours themselves recall Venice: tawny reds, like the brick of a palazzo wall, pinks and a profusion of white predominate; but there is one great difference that the most passionate lover of Venice must concede: the air of the Cypress Gardens, unlike that of the back-canals, is delicious with the scent of flowers.

Mr and Mrs Benjamin Kittredge's garden lies twenty-four miles north of Charleston on the Cooper River: the other two Charleston gardens, Magnolia and Middleton, are on the Ashley. It is a comparatively new garden, having been started as recently as 1927 by Mr Kittredge's father. Originally the gardens formed a part of the great Dean Hall estate, which before the Civil War employed five hundred slaves raising rice. A secluded lake, in which grew a thick cypress forest, was drawn on to flood the rice fields, and an elaborate system of channels and embankments was devised over the years to allow pure water to flow to every corner of the enormous property. After the Civil War and emancipation, the slaves fled, the estate fell into decay and abandon, and soon the forest greedily reclaimed the ground it had lost: the dykes and embankments crumbled, and soon all was desolation. As Mr Lanning Roper, the well-known American authority on gardens, has written, 'What had been a miracle

Now extinct, the Carolina paroquet, used until recently to be seen in the Charleston gardens

of good husbandry became once more a veritable wilderness.'

The owner of the Dean Hall Estate in 1927 was Mr Benjamin Kittredge's father, and it was his inspired idea to use the dense growth of cypress and the black water of the lake as a backdrop and mirror for plantings of azaleas. As in Magnolia Gardens, the cypresses in Mr Kittredge's garden are bearded and festooned with grey Spanish Moss, *Tillandsia usneoides*, which is so typical of the South and at once creates an atmosphere of langour and other-worldly beauty. Spanish Moss, incidentally, is not a true parasite like mistletoe, but is epiphytic, and draws the moisture it needs not from its 'host' but from the air around. The cypresses themselves, the *genii loci* of the garden, are, as in the other two Charleston gardens, *Taxodium distichum*, the Swamp or Bald Cypress. It is difficult to see why they should be described as bald as their rich foliage is their greatest beauty, veridian in early spring, and turning, as summer progresses, to a rich foxy red. These are the trees which make the setting for massed plantings of Indian azaleas, *Rhododendron indicum*, and the vibrant coloured Japanese Kurume azaleas. In their forty years in Cypress Gardens, camellias, too, have prospered, and now make great bushes and small trees, carrying their flowers high overhead and all around from November into April.

The boat glides on: the birds that Audubon loved to paint sing up above and flash from tree to tree; the air is heavy with the scent, not only of azaleas, but of *Daphne odora* and *Osmanthus fragrans*, and if the time of year is spring, the banks are golden with drifts of daffodils. High overhead, the interlacing branches of the cypresses pencil a pattern against the sky, which is reflected in the water below. A bridge spans the channel, its balustrade hung with the legend-haunted Cherokee Rose, and its golden-stemmed white flowers brush our faces as we pass below. As in the nave of a Gothic cathedral, the pillared cypresses rise on either side. Some are wreathed in climbing plants striving upwards towards the light; wisteria mingles its purple tassels with the silver moss; two other climbers which rope the trees are the locally named Supple Jack, *Berchemia scandens*, with its snaky shining stems, and the orange trumpeted *Bignonia capreolata*.

Another flower which Mr Lanning Roper particularly recalls at Cypress Gardens is the white cupped *Zephyranthes atamasco*, like a large, but delicate, crocus, which grows along the waterside. As the flowers mature they take on a pinkish tone, and Mr Roper explains that *Atamasco* is an Indian dialect word meaning 'turning red'. 'My first sight in the Cypress Gardens,' he writes, 'of these exquisite flowers is an unforgettable memory, just as the sound of the yellow-throated warbler, the stately red cardinal and the curiously lilting melody of the mocking bird always recalls these early gardening pilgrimages to Charleston planttations.'

RIGHT: *In the Cypress gardens, 'as in the nave of a Gothic cathedral . . .',*
pillared tree stems rise around

Tresco Abbey ISLES OF SCILLY

Exotic plants off the tip of England

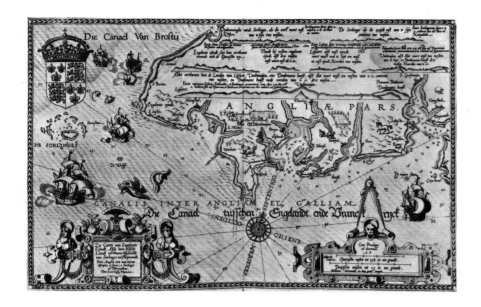

A sixteenth-century Dutch map by Waghaener shows the Isles of Scilly as 'De Sorlinges'

IN JUNE 1866, two months after the end of the Civil War in America, a distinguished, typically Victorian looking gentleman, Lord Proprietor of the Isles of Scilly, wrote about his garden on the island of Tresco to a friend on the mainland, Lady Sophia Tower: 'There has been a cold east wind with a good deal of rain. My garden therefore is very slow in recovering its good looks, and appears yet very seedy and like an invalid. The puya, however, shows one stem for flower, but no aloe as yet; both the *Chamærops excelsa* and *C. humilis* are throwing out large buds; as for dracaenas and beschornerias, I have a forest of both already in full blossom.'

Anyone with any knowledge of the flora of English gardens will notice, from the plants mentioned, that the garden was extraordinary. It is unlikely that the rare puya grew anywhere else out of doors in the British Isles at that time, and the other plants referred to only flower in the most equable of climates.

The island of Tresco is the second largest of the Scilly group, which lie forty miles out in the Atlantic off the Cornish mainland – the nearest English soil to America. The history of the Tresco garden begins in 1834 when Augustus Smith, thirty years younger than when he wrote the letter we have just quoted, leased the islands from the Duchy of Cornwall, then, as now, an appanage of the Crown.

Mr Smith – who was firmly to remain a bachelor all his life – had fallen in love with the romantic Scillies, and with Tresco

LEFT: *Mexican dasylirions flank Neptune's steps with globes of fine-cut spiky foliage*

'*The sea god himself, staring with stony gaze over the flower-filled walks and out to sea.*'

'It is the sea that brings the
Gulf stream to bless the islands...'

Arum lilies by the lily pool

197

in particular, and his love was not to waver for forty years. Tresco was then a wild, almost uninhabited, island, windswept and treeless and barren save for a few poor plants in the parsonage garden which was the only corner where 'the pied flycatcher, the reed warbler and other birds could find some bushes to perch on'. But the island had a magic, described by the Bishop of Truro in a delightful account of Tresco: 'There is a wonderful freshness in the air, and the colours of the white sand, the blue and sapphire sea, the golden seaweed, the Sea Pinks, the Gorse and Heather, have the brightness of a jewel.'

Augustus Smith built himself a house on the rocky ground above the ruins of the twelfth-century Benedictine Monastery, where, it is said, the monks once came in the troublous times of Henry I, as to a sanctuary, 'to save their own souls and to make a garden of God in the midst of the world's wilderness'. The house was stoutly constructed of stone, to withstand the fierce Atlantic gales which sweep Tresco and can do great damage. Its interior in some ways recalls a ship, with bedrooms as narrow and snug as cabins. It was completed in about 1841.

Soon Augustus Smith started to plant trees, first as coverts for game, then as wind-breaks. Nearer his new house he built a high wall, which was to provide shelter for rare plants; for, having come to know the climate of the Scillies, warmed by the Gulf Stream and largely frost-free, he was confident that these would thrive. The collection grew. Plants were sent from Kew, and ships' captains calling at Scilly brought seeds and roots from the most distant parts of the world.

It became Augustus Smith's passion to grow interesting plants, and gradually the garden assumed its present form. This is roughly a rectangle of about twelve acres, sloping to the south, with the new dwelling-house at the top right-hand corner. The garden is divided into three, lengthwise, by the Top Terrace, the shorter Middle Terrace, and at the bottom of the slope, the Long Walk, which is the main axis of the garden, the cross-axis being the Lighthouse Walk, called after the ancient cresset, which came from the island of St Agnes, which stands at its end. This path runs to the Neptune Steps, which lead up to a bust of the sea god himself, staring with stony gaze over the flower-filled walks and out to sea. Numerous paths and flights of steps, cut from the local silvery granite, connect these three main walks.

The gardens at Tresco are famed throughout the world for the rare plants that grow in them, but a lengthy list of names makes tedious reading. More vivid by far are a few delightfully intimate glimpses of how the garden grew – and what grew there – to be found in Augustus Smith's correspondence with Lady Sophia. Wind seemed then, as now, the only problem:

9 May, 1850. Scilly is very gay, and still more so, could you take a walk in my garden, though the winds have played sad havoc there of late, breaking and shrivelling the ixias, sparaxises, and mesem-

The tender beschorneria grows at Tresco

Mexican dasylirions

Puyas grow at Tresco as they do nowhere else in Britain

The exotic outlines of dasylirion and puya

bryanthemums most cruelly; of these last I have now two of the great large-leaved ones in flower, one being a beautiful yellow, and the other a purple, both as large as Adelaide's face.

13 October, 1850. My garden is still in high beauty, and will soon have a fine show of chrysanthemums. At present, the Guernsey Lilies, lately imported from Mr Luff at Guernsey, are pre-eminent; they are very handsome, but are nothing to the *Bella Donnas* as to making a show in the garden. I wish I could send you some of my Red Mullets; I have had so many lately that I have hardly known what to do with them, and of enormous size.

In the intervals of feasting on mullet and cultivating mesembryanthemums with flowers 'as large as Adelaide's face' (Adelaide must have had a small face, for even in the Isles of Scilly mesembryanthemum flowers seldom grow more than four inches across), Smith found time to represent Truro in the House of Commons. But he always spent as much time as he could at Tresco, although the journey from Westminster took infinitely longer in those days than it does today, depending on the direction and force of the wind.

3 September, 1857. On Saturday was wafted over and landed on these shores in 4½ hours. The aloe was conspicuous even on landing, being backed from that point by the greenhouse roof; it has grown of late, and is not so tall as I had expected, being under thirty feet; it is now coming into perfection, the flowers just bursting.

A giant aloe, in a setting of echiums and Phoenix canariensis palm trees at semi-tropical Tresco

Augustus Smith, that 'busy, thoughtful and resolute man', as an obituary notice described him, died in 1872. All the rare plants he cultivated a hundred years ago still flourish in the garden at Tresco, which is now owned by his great-grandnephew, Lt-Commander Dorrien-Smith, who in spite of labour shortages has managed to keep the gardens in a high state of perfection. These are some of the rare plants which Commander Dorrien-Smith indicates to visitors to Tresco with special pride. On the East Rockery, a natural out-crop of rock below the present Tresco Abbey itself, some beautiful Ratas from New Zealand, *Metrosideros robusta*, which are covered with coppery scarlet brushes of flower at the end of June. The rare Ratas are in fact, a feature of Tresco, and elsewhere in the garden grows *M. diffusa* with rosy scarlet stamens, as well as what is probably the largest specimen of *M. tomentosa* in Europe: the Maori name for this tree is Pohutukawa and it is a splendid sight when it flowers in July. Near the first group of *M. robusta*, visitors are shown an extraordinary plant from Mexico – *Furcraea longaeva*, like a large yucca, which after many years' preparation throws up a flower spike of cream and green flower bells which is twenty feet high.

In a part of the garden called Mexico numerous rare succulents are grown, many of which recall similar plants grown in the Huntington garden shown elsewhere in this book, but perhaps the most showy of the plants grown there are the echiums, the giant borages from the Canary Islands and Madeira, which flower in many brilliant shades of blue. *E. scilloniensis* is a natural hybrid which originated in the Isles of Scilly.

Other fascinating plants in the Tresco garden are the pink belled correas from Australia, the climbing Aki-Aki, *Muehlenbeckia complexa* of New Zealand and the silver pink proteas, probably grown nowhere else in the British Isles, which are the great beauties of the flora of South Africa, the strange *Beschorneria yuccoides* from Mexico, the violet pea-flowered *Podalyria calyptrata* from the Cape, and *Myrtus lamu* the Chilean Tree Myrtle, with its dark foliage and strange yellow trunk.

These are only some of the botanical treasures of the plant collection at Tresco; but before leaving this magnificent garden, so well maintained by its present owner in spite of ever-changing conditions, the visitor must see the interesting little museum near the southern entrance of the garden. This is called Valhalla and contains figure-heads of nearly seventy ships which have been wrecked on the rocky coast of Scilly. The influence of the sea is strongly felt at Tresco. It is the sea that brings the Gulf Stream to bless the islands and make a garden such as Tresco possible: for in spite of the occasional gales and very occasional frosts, Scilly has a radiant climate; a climate which can coax botanical rarities, as well as daffodils, which are grown in millions for the London market, 'to take the winds of March with beauty'.

Aloes grow by a garden seat

'Valhalla', containing figure heads of nearly seventy ships wrecked on the coast of the Isles of Scilly

LEFT: *A rocky bank is clothed with flowers and rosettes of giant houseleeks*

Powerscourt COUNTY WICKLOW

An Irish garden in the great tradition

Pegasus caracolling against the Irish sky

SOME MILES SOUTH OF DUBLIN, on the lower slopes of the Wicklow Mountains, lies the demesne – lovely Irish word – of Powerscourt. The site of the present house has been inhabited since the early fourteenth century, when a member of the great family of de la Poer built a castle there, and gave it his name. Three centuries later, after being held in turn by the Irish O'Tooles and English Talbots, Powerscourt passed, in the reign of James I and VI, to Sir Richard Wingfield, ancestor of the Powerscourt family who only recently sold the estate to Mr R. C. B. Slazenger, the present owner. The garden at Powerscourt, though robust with its own character, echoes in several curious ways some other gardens we illustrate in this book. Its magnificent situation recalls Bodnant; some of its statues, the prancing Pegasi especially, remind the visitor of the Parnassus in the garden at Veitshöchheim; and the urns which beautify the terraces at Powerscourt were modelled on those at Bagatelle.

The magnificent house was built by the Viscount Powerscourt of 1743, and the architect is said to have been the German born Richard Cassel, who was author of several great Georgian houses in Ireland. Its façades of silver granite are imposing, and as in other large houses of the period, extend lengthily on either side of the main block, in wings which incorporate stables and outbuildings. At either end of the north front soar slender obelisks,

RIGHT: *The grandiose lay-out of the garden, stretching down to the lake with its twin Pegasi, and the 'comely profile' of the Sugar Loaf Mountain*

on which stone eagles perch. But it is the south façade, less imposing architecturally but oddly satisfying and suitable all the same, which overlooks the gardens, the glory of Powerscourt.

These were laid out, and brought to their present perfection by the sixth and seventh Lords Powerscourt in the last century. Their aim was to give the house, with its splendid view towards the Wicklow hills and the comely profile of the Sugar Loaf Mountain, a setting that was worthy of it, and to provide a frame for the panorama which it overlooks. They had the finest possible material: the lovely Wicklow hills beyond – with their ever-changing light and colour, and their romantic skyline; nearer at hand lay a sharp fall in ground to the south which must have seemed to ask to be sculpted into formal terraces and politer slopes. There was water, too, in the form of the unclassically named Juggy's Pond, waiting to be formalized into an imposing *pièce d'eau*, and later rechristened the Triton Pool.

The first stone of the new terraces was laid in 1843. Their architect, according to Christopher Hussey, was 'a brilliant but dissolute character named Daniel Robertson, who had one day to be concealed in the roof from bailiffs, and owing to severe gout had to be usually transported about the grounds in a wheelbarrow equipped with a bottle of sherry. His inspiration is said to have lasted as long as his daily bottle, after which he flagged ...'

Following the early death of the fifth Lord Powerscourt in 1844, the garden-work flagged too, and it was not actively resumed until about 1858, when his son came of age. But from then it went on apace: the terraces were completed, as was the great piece of ornamental water, Juggy's Pond no longer, which now reflects so lucidly the scudding Irish clouds. The first terrace below the house, lying east and west, is all of eight hundred feet long. From here the main north-south axis of the garden leads downwards towards the Triton Pool, by way of a broad but shallow flight of steps between two noble statues. These steps mark the central cross-axis of the garden, and descend to a wide lawn, which merges at either end with mown *vertugades* or grassy slopes which echo the lawns at Courances. Beyond this central *tapis vert* is a feature which is the hub of the whole garden-plan at Powerscourt, and pleasingly takes the eye, whether the observer is standing on the topmost terrace looking down over the gardens towards the distant view, or if he is looking up at the house from below the terraces. This is the perron, balustraded in black and gold wrought-iron, with its effective pebble-work flooring and graceful ramps on either side. On its southern façade there is a fountain, and over it a sundial: on either side of these are statues of Eolus, God of the Winds. These statues have an interesting history: they originated in the seventeenth

The Bamberg Gate 'which would not be out of place at Veitshöchheim'

Over the graceful ironwork of the perron the view stretches to the lake with its pair of Pegasi, supporters of the Powerscourt arms; and the distant Wicklow mountains

The north façade of Powerscourt terminates in slender obelisks. The German-born Richard Cassel is said to have been the architect

LEFT: *The English Gate, with the crest of the Powerscourt family: three pairs of wings, 'argent on bend gules'*

century in the palace in North Italy of the Duke of Litta: from there they passed into the collection of Prince Napoleon, 'Plon-Plon', who married the daughter of the King of Italy, and took them to Paris. After the fall of the Second Empire, Prince Napoleon, in whose garden at the Palais Royal the statues had stood, sold them to Lord Powerscourt: Christopher Hussey, in writing of Powerscourt, recalls that at the time he wrote: '*Au Palais Royal les Eoles jettaient du gaz par les bouches et de l'eau entre leur jambes: c'était original et joli, un peu baroque.*'

Baroque indeed, and the Eoli, though they breathe fire no longer, look well in their new Irish home – in their delightfully architected framework of Glencree granite and wrought-iron. This was conjured for the seventh Lord Powerscourt about 1870, a period not marked for its good taste, by Francis Cranmer, antiquary to the Royal Academy and a recognized authority on the occultations of the stars and solar eclipses.

From the perron, by way of the cobbled ramps (the pebbles were obtained from the beach at Bray), the descent is continued to the eminence which overlooks the pool. From here five further terraces, like the galleries of a theatre, linked with flights of steps, lead downwards to a grille on either side of which are twin Pegasi, their gallant wings sharp against the iridescent waters of the pool.

What makes the gardens at Powerscourt so remarkable is their grandeur of scale combined, as so rarely happens, with great delicacy and refinement of detail. Their setting is superb, but their design and their execution are worthy of it. Meticulously kept, again rare for an Irish garden, every part of the gardens rewards the closest study. We have examined the perron in some

205

Mellow stone and distant views delight the eye at Powerscourt

Over the perron fountain at Powerscourt a sundial only tells the sunny hours ('Horas non numero nisi serenas'). On either side are puffing Aeoli which once adorned the Palais Royal

A diminutive sentinel blows a sad salute

A giant urn, more than eight feet high, one of several on the great terrace at Powerscourt, with a statue of Diana the Huntress beyond

RIGHT: *A ruminative Water God looks across Triton's Pool, towards a planting of trees, cedars, ilexes and wellingtonias*

POWERSCOURT

A pair of Dragon Trees (Dracaena draco), delicate save in the gentlest climate

An avenue of Monkey Puzzles (araucaria); an imposing planting

detail: but there are a dozen features at Powerscourt which deserve scrutiny: the Pegasi themselves are unusual, being cast in zinc; the bronze groups of Amorini on the perron were designed by the eighteenth-century French sculptor, Joseph Marin, better known for his work in terra-cotta. Many of the urns on the balustrade of the upper terrace were taken from the original moulds of urns at Versailles, and came to Powerscourt through the good offices of Sir Richard Wallace, who had had them copied for his garden at Bagatelle.

There is also at Powerscourt an old walled garden, which was in existence long before the great developments of the southern terrace were carried out a hundred years ago. This garden is beautified by a number of graceful gates of wrought-iron, among them the English Gate, lacy and delicate, between urn-capped piers; the Vine Gate, of Italian workmanship, consisting of iron wrought in a vine-leaf design; and the Bamberg Gate, which would not be out of place at Veitshöchheim or Schwetzingen, and came from Bamberg Cathedral: this gate has a particularly charming baroque air, and is in a *trompe l'oeil* perspective design, surmounted with an elaborate scroll-work, and a vase of iron flowers.

The gardens at Powerscourt, and its immediate surroundings, are splendidly timbered: within the confines of the garden grow a thirty-foot high *Drimys winteri*, aromatic cousin of the magnolias, and a Blue Gum, *Eucalyptus globulus*, which in its short forty years of life has shot up a hundred feet or more. In the woody area below the Triton Pool grows the tallest tree in all Ireland, a Sitka Spruce. Elsewhere in the demesne there is a grove of Monkey Puzzles, *Araucaria imbricata*, which are so seldom grown in groups but are highly impressive with their dome-like tops of glossy green and ram-rod glaucous stems.

Powerscourt is a magnificent example of an aristocratic garden laid out with taste, knowledge and imagination. As we have seen, its situation and its exquisite details make it outstanding. It is extraordinary, too, in that it is probably the last garden of its size and quality ever to have been created. When it was completed in the 1870's, change was already in the air: garden design was soon to pass from the hands of the architects and artist into the hands of the horticulturalist: green-fingers are more adept with a trowel or pruning knife than with the set-square, and what had been the pastime of kings and noblemen was soon to become a hobby for the amateur horticulturalist.

The thousands of visitors who admire the splendid perspectives of Powerscourt every year, for it is open for all to see, should pay tribute to the taste and munificence of the Powerscourt family for providing Ireland with so fine a pleasure-ground. It is good to know that, under the new régime of Mr and Mrs Slazenger it will continue to offer a place of recreation and refreshment to all who go there.

RIGHT: *The pebble paved floor of the perron at Powerscourt: beyond lie towering trees and the Wicklow mountains*

Bodnant NORTH WALES

A splendid combination of terraces and shrubs

THE GARDEN AT BODNANT IN Denbighshire has been described as the first garden of Britain, and with justification, for surely nowhere else can be found together all the qualities which make the perfect garden. Its site is a romantic valley falling to the south, with Snowdon, Britain's grandest mountain-range, beyond. The soil is well watered, and the trees and plants which fill its six great terraces, and the green leaf-canopied glen below, are the finest that three generations of great gardeners have chosen, confident that they will thrive in the climate of North Wales. A visit to Bodnant is memorable to a gardener and plant-lover for the taste and garden-science that he finds displayed there; but it is equally memorable to someone who has no knowledge of plants and horticulture for the visual delight of colour and splendid panoramas that everywhere greet his eye.

The gardens at Bodnant are the creation of the first Lady Aberconway, her son and grandson, now President of that august body, the Royal Horticultural Society, as his father was before him. Work on the gardens was started in 1875, and ever since constant care and imaginative affection have been lavished on them. In 1949 they were endowed by the late Lord Aberconway and given to the National Trust, the guardian of so many of Britain's beautiful domains; so their future is assured, all the more so since the present Lord Aberconway and his wife take such an enthusiastic interest in their administration and imaginative development.

On leaving the garden entrance of the house and stepping on to the first of the terraces which lie to the south-west, the grandest view greets the visitor. Beyond the garden, which we will visit terrace by terrace, on the far side of the Conway Valley, lies the noble outline of the Snowdon range; in the middle distance plantations of high trees on the further slopes of the garden frame the view, and lead the eye towards the not-far-distant mountains. These plantings, mostly of firs, a few oaks and an underplanting of flowering trees, are particularly beautiful in spring, when they seem to clothe the steep slopes of the valley with a brocade of ever-changing light and shade.

Bodnant is famous for its rhododendrons

LEFT: '*The great lily-pond, bowed outward*'

Below the first terrace, paved and planted with roses, presided over by a pair of surprised looking sphinxes and two red-stemmed arbutus, lies a terrace which is used as a croquet lawn. It is approached down neat steps which divide and descend on either side of an elaborate baroque fountain, curtained in early summer with the white tassels of *Wistaria venusta* and *Wistaria sinensis alba*: the edge of the croquet-lawn terrace, sheltered by a high wall, is planted with several fine specimens of interesting shrubs, such as *Eucryphia nymansensis*, with the attractive dwarf lilac, *Syringa microphylla*, growing below, and a vast cushion of the rosy-purple flowered, low-growing *Daphne tangutica*. Over the creeper-clad wooden balustrade of the terrace we see the great lily pond on the third terrace, bowed outwards towards the south, and planted with many rare nymphaeas in shades of white and cream and crimson: softening the formal edge of the pool are clumps of ornamental reeds and eulalias. This terrace is bordered with a loose but luxuriant hedge of *Erica stricta*. But the real *genii loci* here are the two great cedars, both planted in 1876, one at either end, round which the terrace was designed in 1914. One is a magnificent specimen of *Cedrus atlantica glauca*, a pyramid of frosty blue foliage, and the other, *Cedrus libani*, the green Cedar of Lebanon. As on the croquet-lawn terrace, the wall on the other side of the lily-pond terrace offers grateful shelter to tender plants, such as the unusual rosy-belled *Buddleia colvilei*, *Photinia glomerata* and the lovely pink *Camellia reticulata*. Below them grow several sweet-scented delicate plants of rhododendron, and the border is edged with the lilac-flowered *Liriope muscari*, which occurs throughout the formal part of the gardens at Bodnant, and provides a haze of purple flowers in late summer.

The fourth terrace is gained by twin flights of shallow grey-green stone steps wreathed with that attractive member of the potato family, *Solanum crispum*, in its best variety, 'Glasnevin', with its myriad blue flowers all summer through. The steps hug the southern wall of the terrace, and lead one down to a rose garden, neatly bedded and pathed, and decorated with sturdy pergolas of trellis-work, capped with wooden urns, the design for which was taken, unexpectedly enough, from those in the garden of the Ritz Hotel in London. Here grow, as well as roses, a lofty *Eucalyptus gunnii* planted in 1916, and the attractive yellow *Clematis tangutica*: and nearby are two smaller gardens within-the-garden, one given over entirely to white flowers, and the other to flaunting Tree peonies, including many of the Saunders hybrid which we also see in the garden at Winterthur in the United States.

Descending further, the visitor now reaches the fifth terrace, along the length of which, and parallel to the terraces above, lies the canal, with, at one end, the most enchanting architectural feature of the garden at Bodnant, the Pin Mill. Some time before the Second World War broke out, Lord and Lady Aber-

The canal, with the Green Theatre at the further end

On the topmost terrace, a fine French stone vase with a statue of Priapus beyond

LEFT: *The Pin Mill at the end of the canal, lending real enchantment to the view*

BODNANT

Fountain, foliage and a sunlit façade

A baroque fountain, curtained in wisteria

The gabled Pin Mill with, in the foreground, a sphinx and a columnar cypress
The 'frosty blue foliage' of Cedrus atlantica glauca laps the lily pond

A view over the Bodnant garden towards the Snowdon range

A miniature waterfall in the dell

conway acquired, in Gloucestershire, a beautiful little building, a gazebo dating from 1730, which had fallen on evil days, having sunk from being the elegant appendage of a country house belonging to the King family, to being used as a tannery and as a factory for making pins. The Aberconways re-erected it at Bodnant, where its gabled wings, tower with its ogival roof and façade enriched with the King arms and swags of flowers, now reflect themselves in the still waters of the canal, lending real enchantment to the scene. The canal terrace is bordered on one side with a rich bed of herbaceous plants, in tones of grey-blue and purple: while in the 'dry' wall behind flourishes a plant which is a feature of the garden at Bodnant, and which anywhere else would be considered a rarity, *lewisia*, which star the stonework with their motley, chintzy flowers of red and white stripes. At the north end of the canal terrace from the Pin Mill, is a raised stage of smooth turf, almost a *Théâtre de Verdure*, such as the one at Marlia, with wings of clipped yew, and a pair of baroque statues.

The sixth of the terraces is planted with magnolias in many varieties; one of the late Lord Aberconway's maxims was, 'Find out what plants grow well for you and plant a lot of them'. Here is evidence of that excellent advice, and *MM. kobus, salicifolia robusta* and many others, glorify this part of the garden in spring, to be followed by the later flowering *sieboldii, wilsonii* and *sinensis*. Beyond the magnolias, the path dives deep down the valley's slope, and into a sea of plants that thrive in half-shade, such as the rarer rhododendrons and azaleas. The garden here changes character completely: formality is done with, naturalistic planting begins; and yet the same meticulous taste holds sway, and the planting is instinct with the knowledge that leaf-forms must be contrasted, that masses of colour should supplement each other; and that value should be set on the architectural quality of plants. This is also the type of planting found in the woodland areas that run at right angles to the terraces, on either side of the steep paths which follow the same incline. On one side a stream tumbles down the slope, and, as might have been expected, this natural asset has been fully utilized, its flow being caught, here in a series of moss-bordered pools, and there allowed to fall sparkingly over a miniature water-fall. Its banks are planted with the plants that love the waterside and cool damp soil for their roots. Primulas raise their coloured candelabra around, and the blue Himalayan poppy, *Meconopsis betonicifolia*, flaunts its flowers against a background of azaleas and camellias, and shaded by the magnolias which Lord Aberconway's father loved so well. Nearby is a weir, surmounted by a neatly railed bridge which in summer is fringed with wisteria, while standing grandly by is the loftiest tree of the gardens of Bodnant, *Abies grandis*, the Californian Fir.

Before we leave Bodnant, mention must be made of the mausoleum high up on a leafy crag, built by Lord Aberconway's great-grandfather, Mr Pochin. From there, we pass through groves of rare trees, among them *arbutus* and *embothriums*, a speciality at Bodnant, and approach the house once more, past borders of shrubs, until, by means of the oval Yew Garden, part of the original garden, we gain the Round Garden, and a measure of formality once more: for the Round Garden is planted to a loose plan with daphnes, dwarf rhododendrons and ericas, and has as its centre a graceful scallopped fountain in the form of a dolphin, a new and delightful addition. Further on, beyond the rock-garden, is an arch of laburnums which makes a shimmering tunnel of gold in May, a most striking sight.

Those great English horticultural experts, A. G. L. Hellyer and Christopher Hussey, have written:

> The great genius displayed throughout Bodnant . . . has been in the combination of mass with texture, architectural sense with horticultural science. There are other gardens where particular *genera* are cultivated with possibly equal success, and other gardens of which the architecture and landscape may be not inferior. But it can be claimed that there is none in which so many *genera* are so superbly grown and displayed together with such a sense of their being parts of a great whole, predominantly natural, but man-made in detail and design. It is profoundly revealing of the national genius, as shaped through two centuries of visual and horticultural development, to compare Bodnant with such a grand Continental garden as Villandry – where the synthesis is the exact reverse.

Rhododendrons in the dell

'An arch of laburnums . . . a tunnel of gold in May'

Old Westbury LONG ISLAND

Echoes of the Edwardian era outside New York

ABOUT FORTY-FIVE MINUTES in time from the heart of New York –
but how very much further in spirit – lie the gardens of Westbury House, one of the oldest properties in Long Island. Its
ownership can be traced back to its original purchase from
the Indians. Some of the trees which shade the large and beautifully planned garden are recorded by the Long Island Horticultural Society as being the largest and oldest of their species on
Long Island. They give an air of repose and maturity to a garden on which the creators have lavished for half a century every
blessing that taste, knowledge and a great fortune can bestow.

Westbury House itself, a polite pastiche of the early Georgian
style by the English architect George Crawley, was built in
1906. Its walls are of rosy brick, faded to the colour of pot-
pourri, with limestone for the facings and grey-gold Rutland
stone for the high-pitched, dormered roof. The house stands
well, on the top of rising ground, in leafy parkland, with twin
avenues of beech and linden running to north and south. Inside
is a fine collection of eighteenth-century English furniture and
pictures, which visitors can also enjoy; and, indoors, they will
find the same taste and knowledge displayed, as they discover
outdoors in the layout of the gardens themselves.

In 1958 the gardens and house were endowed by the J. S.
Phipps Foundation, which desired to maintain the garden as an
Arboretum and Horticultural Collection and the house as a
Museum, their aim being to preserve the beauty and very per-
sonal charm of the whole place in the tradition established by
Mrs John S. Phipps, and to show future generations how a great
estate of the early twentieth century looked.

On arrival, the visitor to Old Westbury passes through an area
of green lawns, shaded with great trees, and skirting the house
to the westward side, descends steps towards the smaller of the
two pieces of water. At hand grows one of the original specimen
trees, a lofty Brittle Willow, *Salix fragilis*. Beyond lies the box-
wood garden, its formal shape outlined in ancient box: in its
centre lies a pond of tropical lilies to reflect a Grecian colonnade
which is an ornament of this part of the garden. Proceeding to-

*Primulas, forget-me-nots and white azaleas in a wild
corner of the garden*

LEFT: *Pink dogwoods frame a view of Westbury House*

Paths, pergola and terracing make the plan at Old Westbury

A rustic pergola over a neat path of old bricks

Sweet-williams, iris and canterbury bells in an informally planted border

221

LEFT: *Light blossoms contrasting with an ancient fir*

wards the Italian garden, which is the most spectacular garden-within-a-garden at Old Westbury, two more historical trees are passed – an ancient red maple, *Acer rubrum*, and a Japanese white pine *Pinus parviflora*. The Italian garden always presents a scene of brilliant colour through the spring, summer and autumn, and is replanted every month to keep the display going. Every shade of tulip is succeeded by a gay tapestry of annuals and as autumn approaches the beds brim over with chrysanthemums. It is here, in the Italian garden, that every year the newest, strongest growing and most rewarding new strains of flowers are presented. Here too, there is a pond of hardy lilies, baroque in shape, and at the south end of the garden a pergola which is particularly beautiful in spring, when it is wreathed in wisteria, the serpentine grey stems of which rise from a bank of Japanese Iris.

Leaving the sunshine and colour of the Italian garden, the visitor next passes through a Pinetum whose sombre shade prepares him for the romantic gloom of the Ghost Walk, a dark tunnel of Hemlock, *Tsuga canadensis*, modelled on one which Mrs Phipps knew years ago at Battle Abbey in Sussex. Emerging

A carpet of blue ageratum before a rose hung pergola

Wisteria drapes the terrace wall

222

into the sunshine once more, he finds the rose garden – typically English, with its box-bordered rose-beds. Then he follows the colourful Primrose Walk leading to the charming English cottage garden. Striking right, the great lawn lying to the south of the house is crossed: from here the house itself looks very handsome, and seems to breathe the comfort and security of its age which is the equivalent of the Edwardian era in England. Vined and creepered, pillared and generously fenestrated, it seems to smile a welcome over its balustrade. Garden-parties are nothing new to Old Westbury, and one seems to catch a whiff of cigar-smoke as well as the scent of perfectly mown grass. To the east lies the lake, which, with the green woodland around it, might be in any park in Shropshire.

At Old Westbury, the Phipps family has tried to make a series of pleasure gardens rather than a stiff and formidable collection of botanical specimens. They have aimed at creating a feeling of beauty and general interest rather than a living text-book on plants and plant materials. How well they have succeeded any visitor to Old Westbury will see.

Geraniums fill the urns on the terrace steps

The Huntington

BOTANICAL GARDENS, CALIFORNIA

Rare plants around a famous art collection

The seventeenth-century Italian temple with its wrought-iron dome and 'Venus with Cupid' by F. G. Villa

A TENUOUS THREAD OF ASSOCIATION, memory and sentiment connects the name of San Marino, the tiny republic in Italy, with the Henry E. Huntington Library, Art Gallery and Botanical Gardens in California. James de Barth Shorb, the original owner of the site some fifteen miles from Los Angeles, remembered his boyhood home in Maryland which his grandfather, finding that the acreage of his property was exactly the same as that of the independent State of San Marino, had named after it. So James de Barth Shorb also called his estate in California San Marino.

There he built the neat, two-storey Victorian house set among orchards of citrus trees that we see in the print of 1880. The name no longer pertains to the property that was the old San Marino Ranch, but is perpetuated in the name of the city in which the Huntington Botanical Gardens are situated.

In 1892, Henry Edwards Huntington visited the Shorb Ranch while en route to San Francisco from his home in New York. Something of its location and beautiful views south across the San Gabriel Valley and west to the setting sun, must have stayed in his mind, for ten years later he bought the estate. Then, under the direction of William Hertrich who for the next fifty years was to be in charge of the developing of the Huntington Gardens, Mr Huntington's plans for the conversion of the old San Marino Ranch began. This present description of the Gardens owes much to Mr Hertrich's delightful personal recollections, published in 1949, as it also does to the Huntington Library's admirable *Visitor's Guide to the Library, Art Gallery and Gardens*.

The old Shorb house was demolished in 1906 and two years later the foundations were laid for the residence where from 1914 Mr and Mrs Huntington were to live. The house was an elegant, cool-looking Georgian-Colonial building, pillared and porticoed, and set in an exquisite landscape. To the north lies the noble line of the Sierra Madre mountains, with two of Southern California's celebrated peaks – Mount Wilson and Mount Lowe. In the far distance, north-eastward, on clear days

RIGHT: *The north vista, which runs towards the Sierra Madre mountains*

may be seen Mount San Antonio, locally known as Old Baldy. To the south is the San Gabriel Valley and to the south-east lie the blue distances of the Whittier hills. This was the background which awaited the gardens that were to be.

Although the new house was built primarily as a home for Mr and Mrs Huntington, it was also to provide a setting for many of the treasures which Mr Huntington collected. There, during his lifetime, he was surrounded by his paintings, the great portraits of the British eighteenth-century school, and by examples of English and French decorative arts which he accumulated through the years. On the founder's death in 1927 the home became the Art Gallery, and here the art treasures – most famous of which is perhaps Gainsborough's *The Blue Boy* – are on public display. Across the lawn from the Art Gallery is the Library building, completed in 1920 when Mr Huntington brought his priceless collections of books and manuscripts there from New York. The previous year he had made over the botanical gardens and his collections in trust as a free and privately endowed institution for the use of all qualified persons and in 1928 the exhibits and gardens were opened to the public. To give an idea of the importance of the collection of rare books and manuscripts, one of the most famous in the world, it is only necessary to mention that those which are on public exhibit include manuscripts such as the Ellesmere Chaucer (1410) and such rare printed books as the Gutenberg Bible (1450–55) and the first folio edition of Shakespeares' collected plays. But the unique quality of the Huntington Art Gallery and Library is that their priceless contents are set in a garden which itself is full of rarities: it is as if the Wallace Collection were housed at Kew, or the Carnavalet at Bagatelle.

Thus, when the visitor has viewed the paintings in the Art Gallery, he may step onto its south terrace and, if the weather is clear on a winter day, be greeted with a distant view of the snow-topped peaks of San Jacinto and Cucamonga rising above the golden, sun-drenched Californian countryside. Closer at hand, lie the gardens where grow rare and exotic plants, collected from the four corners of the earth. Near the Art Gallery the Moreton Bay Chestnut, *Castanospermum australe*, native to Australia, casts its welcome shade, while under Sago Palms from Japan, a balustrade is wreathed with the golden goblet flowers of Copa de Oro from Mexico. Nearby are several species of African Coral Trees, *erythrina*, which bear a profusion of red flowers in winter and early spring. The North Vista leads the eye towards the great Italian Renaissance fountain of Istrian stone in the form of three great shells borne aloft by spouting dolphins. On either side of the grass-covered vista are fern-bordered paths which wind away through plantings of rhododendrons, camellias and azaleas, all shaded by California live oaks, *Quercus agrifolia*.

In the far north-west section of the two-hundred acre gardens, in a grove of orange trees, stands the Founder's Mausoleum,

Exotic philodendron leaves contrast with their marble vase

planted about with some of Henry Huntington's favourite trees; east of it lies an avocado orchard, one of the first to be planted in America. The Mausoleum is simple and distinguished, with its Ionic pillars and peaceful setting. Designed by John Russell Pope, it was the prototype for his famous work, the Jefferson Memorial in Washington.

A charming part of the gardens is the Shakespeare Garden, one of the newest features, paved and sundialled, with a bust of the poet overlooking the peaceful scene. This garden is planted only with flowers mentioned in the plays, a delightful fancy, where Perdita could well exclaim:

> Here's flowers for you;
> Hot lavender, mints, savory, marjoram;
> The marigold, that goes to bed wi' the sun,
> And with him rises weeping.

To the south stands one of the original survivors from the old Shorb Ranch – a lofty Kauri pine, *Agathis australe*, from Australia, as unlike the pines known to us as one can imagine. Here, too, grow some ferny Montezuma cypresses, which William Hertrich raised from seed imported from Mexico, and planted in 1909 in the nursery he had established to propagate trees for his planting programme. And in this part of the garden, too, is the Temple of Love, which once stood in a garden in the vicinity of Versailles and which contains the stone statue '*Love, the Captive of Youth*' attributed to Simon Boizot (1743–1809).

It is difficult to enumerate the exotic trees which have been planted or raised in the Huntington Gardens; just a few are the rare Toog Tree from Africa, the showy Chinese Fringe Tree, the Surinam Cherry, *Eugenia uniflora*, and the Australian Bottle Tree, *Brachychiton populneum*, with its pearly clusters of flowers.

A fascinating corner of the gardens, and one of the first to be completed, is that devoted to the lily ponds. Here are elaborately designed pools in which grow rare lilies and graceful lotus. Beyond the lily ponds, on the other side of the drive, lies what is perhaps the most striking feature of the Huntington gardens, the Cactus Garden. Ten acres, containing 25,000 plants, constitute the largest collection in the world of mature desert plants growing out of doors. When, nearly fifty years ago, Mr Hertrich suggested such a garden to Mr Huntington, his employer was unenthusiastic, his only knowledge of the genus having been a painful encounter with a cactus in the early days of his career, while supervising work for the Southern Pacific railroad in Arizona. Mr Hertrich, undeterred, explained that the climate of Southern California would be perfect for such a garden, which would be the first of its kind in the world, and of the greatest educational value. Thus the Cactus Garden came into being.

THE HUNTINGTON
BOTANICAL GARDENS

How the site of the Huntington Botanical Gardens looked in 1880

The main gates came from Bedington Park in Surrey
The Japanese garden with its vermilion bridge

One other part of the grounds deserves mention: the Japanese Garden. Here a half-moon bridge, of bright vermilion, arches over a pond, planted all around with maples, pines, azaleas and wisteria. On the western slope of this Garden, shadowed by oaks, are five acres of camellias, a collection comprising more than a thousand varities of *sasanquas, japonicas,* and *reticulatas.* Nearby stands an authentic Japanese tea house, a two-storied building of the Meiji period, first brought to the gardens when Mr Hertrich in 1912 transformed an unsightly canyon into what is now the Japanese Garden. About five years ago the tea house, restored and furnished under the supervision of a well known Japanese artist, was opened to public view for the first time. Visitors may not enter, but when the screens forming the outer walls are drawn back the beautiful rooms with their Japanese appointments and traditional flower arrangements are delightfully exposed on two sides and can be observed from the encircling path.

The Huntington Botanical Gardens are among the most important in America, and for several reasons: new methods of garden work were first tried out there, such as the transportation of fully-grown trees – now an established craft in the United States; under the direction of Mr Hertrich, now Curator Emeritus, rare and precious plants by the thousand have been raised there; others have been preserved in cultivation, like the Wine Palm from Chile which is nearly extinct in its native land, and the desert-plant garden has set an example which has been copied all over the world.

Henry Edwards Huntington, that great and generous American gentleman, lies quietly in the midst of the beauty he created and left to the people of California. It is said that he wanted no biography. What he said about his beloved library would apply to his great garden too: 'It represents the reward of all the work I have ever done, and the realization of much happiness.'

RIGHT: *'The desert-plant garden has set an example . . . copied all over the world'*

water lilies and statuary

Classical statuary and high urns of carved marble embellish the garden: the statue of Neptune came from the Hofburg, the palace of the Austrian Emperors

LEFT: *The cactus garden with its palms and columnar cereus plants*

A lily pond with a group of banana trees

Hidcote Manor GLOUCESTERSHIRE

An American's garden in the Cotswolds

WHEN THE LATE LAWRENCE JOHNSTON, an American who had adopted England as his home, first planted his garden at Hidcote nearly sixty years ago, a friend remarked, 'This man is planting his garden as no one else has ever planted a garden before.' It will be our purpose in this description to try to explain why the garden was so different at that time from other English gardens: since then, fortunately for the standard of domestic gardening in England and elsewhere, Hidcote has had many emulators and could be said to have founded a school of gardening which finds more pupils every year.

Hidcote Manor lies in the greenest, quietest corner of England, on the borderline between Worcestershire and Gloucestershire: in a county of curling, deep-set lanes, near the enchanting little towns of Broadway and Chipping Campden: in short, in the Cotswolds. From the garden there is a view over the 'coloured counties' towards Bredon where, one summertime, the bells sounded for Alfred Housman, 'a happy noise to hear'.

Major Lawrence Johnston bought Hidcote Manor in 1907 and at once set about laying out the garden. The site was high, and offered few of those ready-made features which are so helpful when planning a garden from new: there was one good cedar and some fine beeches, but no old walls, in spite of its being in the Cotswolds, which is stone-wall country. What was to be a garden was the barest field, very exposed and windy; the soil was heavy. Major Johnston must have had great imagination to be able to envisage a garden there, and courage not to be daunted by the difficulties involved. He died, alas, some years ago, but not before he had seen his vision realized, and his garden full, luxuriant and mature, and acclaimed as the very best of the smaller gardens in England.

Why did Hidcote achieve, so quickly, its high reputation? First, it seems, because it was differently planted. How? 1907, with England in the full, slightly flushed prosperity of Edwardian days, was certainly the hey-day of the herbaceous border: but there was no conventional herbaceous border at Hidcote; rather did Lawrence Johnston choose to plant shrubs, shrub-

'One of the twin pavilions. . . looking faintly oriental. From their very English paned windows inviting views are to be had of further allées . . .'

LEFT: 'Chubby peacocks in yew, which give the garden character even in the depth of winter'

One border at Hidcote is devoted to shrub roses

The long walk runs south from a brick-bridged fern-bordered stream

roses and herbaceous plants all together, in one border, a combination which was, at that time, quite original and new. V. Sackville-West has written, in a description of the garden at Hidcote, 'We must always remember that the fashion of one generation becomes the commonplace of the next; but that is no reason why we should not pay a grateful tribute to the person who had the first idea.' Many gardeners have been inspired to plant their gardens according to the precepts adopted at Hidcote, with greater or lesser success, but we would say that there is still nothing ordinary about such plantings; they have the advantages not only of attraction, but ease of upkeep too.

There was something else quite original, in England and America, at least, in Lawrence Johnston's planting: something for which he may have drawn inspiration from Italy, a country he loved, knew well and often visited. There is a whisper of Marlia in the garden at Hidcote, in that the garden is planned rather like a house, with 'rooms' opening off a central vista – a master-axis, just as in a palace (for in a garden everything must of course be on a greater scale than in an ordinary house) salons open off a central gallery. These *enfilades* of gardens within-a-garden, make the second great novelty of Hidcote. So we have 'mixed' plantings, as they have come to be called, and outdoor rooms. But rooms, out-of-doors, or in, must have walls, and there are few walls of stone at Hidcote; which brings us to the third quality which makes Hidcote, even after sixty years, so original and 'new' – its hedges: hedges of every different kind of plant, and some of several different kinds planted together to make 'tapestry' hedges. There are yew hedges, each smoothly trimmed into architectural forms – buttresses, pediments and the like. There is one particularly beautiful hedge of copper-beech, which glows like porphyry when the sun strikes it; though regular shearing deprives it of most of its tiny pink flowers, enough are spared to shine like stars among the new pink young growth, when it looks like a Persian painting. There is one hedge of silver euonymus, another of mingled yew and box, the sombre and glistening greens in contrast; and there is another most spectacular hedge in which yew, holly and beech are combined to present in summer a marbled surface of several greens, and in winter one of greens splashed with foxy brown. It is thought that Lawrence Johnston was the first gardener to plant mixed hedges such as these, though for centuries their obvious inspiration, the motley hedges of any country lane, have been there for all to see.

The garden at Hidcote is entered by way of a courtyard, where against the dove-coloured walls of the house grow the purple and gold flowers, cohorts of them, of *Solanum crispum*, exotic cousin of the potato, spicey-leaved choisya, white flowered carpentaria and several rounded bushes, covered with golden buttercups of flower in summer, of the famous *Hypericum patulum*, first raised at Hidcote, and which now bears its name. The en-

The stilt garden: 'high sculpted hedges of hornbeam'

The pool with the great yew pediment beyond

trance to the garden is shadowed by the tall cedar which Lawrence Johnston found before he started to plant the garden. A broad grass walk lies ahead, the main axis: off either side, doors and archways cut in the famous hedges beckon one into smaller gardens: one opening leads to a yew-walled enclosure which is almost entirely filled with a vast circular pond, raised so that the surface of the water is almost waist high, making the large and friendly goldfish it contains seem companionably close. Here the hedges are tall and dark, but enlivened by the brilliant *Tropaeolum speciosum* which does not usually thrive in dry English soil, but only gives of its scarlet best in damper Scotland.

'Mrs Winthrop's Garden', called after Major Johnston's mother, is planted in tones of gold and cream and white: here grow yellow peonies, the golden hop and sword-leaved yuccas raise their steeples of bells over cushions of Ladies Bedstraw, *Alchemilla mollis*; and the scent of evening primroses hangs on the air. Another border is planted in heraldic reds and blues, with *Lychnis chalcedonica* flaming gules against the azure of steel-blue monkshoods.

Another garden-rule well demonstrated at Hidcote is that of planting in the mass. One whole border, for instance, is planted with yellow Esperance peonies, growing with a vigour and splendour that rivals Professor Saunders' magnificent hybrids at Winterthur. One disadvantage, of course, of a border wholly devoted to one plant only, is the fact that when not in flower it can look dull and bare, but this is not so with peonies, as their spring and autumn foliage is so beautiful. But the conscientious gardener should study the habit of the plant he wants to set *en masse*, and remember how it looks when not in flower. Such plantings at Hidcote are those of fuchsias, resplendent in later summer, and of 'old' roses to which a long border is especially devoted. Here are many of the roses which scent the air in the Savill Gardens at Windsor and at Bagatelle. Many have the charming French names which contribute greatly to their *mystique*, like Reine des Violettes, Madame Pierre Oger, Coupe d'Hebe and Boule de Neige. Of the roses at Hidcote, V. Sackville-West has written in her own vibrant style: 'It would take pages to enumerate them all, so let me merely revive the memory of that June day and the loaded air, and the bushes weeping to the ground with the weight of their own bloom, a rumpus of colour, a drunkenness of scents.'

The great grass path which runs down the middle of the garden at Hidcote and makes its main axis is interrupted, after it passes the 'red' border, by a flight of steps of silver stone, creeper-clad, mossy and already mellowed by their sixty years. These lead up towards high sculpted hedges of hornbeam, which frame the view through a gate of wrought iron. On either side stand twin pavilions with peaked ogival roofs, looking faintly Oriental. From their very English paned windows inviting views are to be had of further allées, other bright parterres.

Rosa gallica in a setting of contrasting foliage

LEFT: *The sunk garden with the cedar, the only original feature which Lawrence Johnston found*

Nearby, is another garden such as only a gardener with an artist's eye could have conjured. It is not really a garden at all, but a large, perfectly proportioned stretch of turf, known as the Theatre Lawn, enclosed with a hedge of yew. At one end, on a little rise, stand a group of lofty beeches. If we have likened the different enclosures of the garden at Hidcote to the rooms of a house or palace, this lawn must surely be the ball-room, with a grass-green parquet floor and an orchestra platform at the further end. In its simplicity, its complete reliance on scale and emptiness for its effect, the great lawn at Hidcote reveals, as nothing else does, the planning genius of Lawrence Johnston. In spite, or because, of its simplicity it has a sophisticated Continental air: it might be a garden in the Ile de France, and it could be the background for a group by Lancret or Pater.

This blending of simplicity and sophistication is typical of Hidcote. Nowhere else in the world, except perhaps at Sissinghurst, a much 'younger' garden, does one find rare plants grown in almost 'cottage' settings: the 'cottage' feel of the smaller garden-rooms at Hidcote is given by the topiary – the pinnacles and chubby peacocks of yew which give the garden character,

The theatre lawn relies on scale and emptiness for effect

even in the depths of winter. It is given by the informality of the paving; by the smallness; by the close planting which might almost seem hugger-mugger to anyone who had not tried to copy it; by the way that tall campanula grows almost on the path – was it planted or did it sow itself? Either way, it is there, it looks absolutely right; you would miss it if it were not.

Such is the reputation of Hidcote, and such was the garden science of its creator, who was also a great plant-collector, that several fine plants bear Hidcote's name. We have already mentioned the shrubby St Johns Wort, Hypericum Hidcote Gold, introduced by Lawrence Johnston from China to enrich the gardens of the western world; there is also the rich purple Hidcote lavender and a Hidcote dianthus.

Lawrence Johnston died some years ago. Before his death, however, he gave Hidcote to the National Trust, who administer it in conjunction with the Royal Horticultural Society. Every year it is visited by thousands: all who see the garden must leave it refreshed; many must leave it inspired; a few, very few, may successfully emulate it: it is tempting to any gardener to try, for they could never find a better model.

Close planting under a cherry's branches

Obelisks of yew rise from a bed of tree peonies

Winterthur DELAWARE

Natural gardens on a princely scale

Flowers line the steps from the high terrace at Winterthur

THE NAME WINTERTHUR, now so celebrated in the gardening world, is the name of a village in Switzerland which was once the home of the family of James Antoine Bidermann. James Antoine married the daughter of E. I. du Pont de Nemours from whom the present well-known family of du Pont descends. The Bidermanns, in 1839, built a new house near the powder mill which the du Pont family had founded on the banks of the Brandywine Creek and they called it Winterthur: nearby they laid out a sunken garden. This garden was the tiny seed from which the splendid present gardens grew. Already in 1859 a visitor wrote, 'There is not to be found in the country a more charming and lovely spot'. The 'lovely spot' now covers thirty acres.

The creator of the present Winterthur gardens, which every spring attract thousands of visitors, is the Bidermanns' great nephew, Henry Francis du Pont, who inherited the estate thirty-seven years ago. Since then, he has devoted so much of his time to planning and planting the gardens, that he has come to refer to himself as his own head gardener. Of his talents and taste no visitors who admire the gardens in their present beauty can have any doubts.

Three rules seem to have activated the planning at Winterthur – three excellent precepts which it would be good for any gardener to bear in mind, however small, by comparison, his plot. The first: plant boldly, in large clumps. The second: make full use wherever possible of indigenous trees. And the third: plan every colour scheme with meticulous care.

Regard for these three rules is everywhere apparent. Shrubs, azaleas especially, are planted in drifts of a hundred plants, and native trees, such as Beech Hickory, the red, black and white oaks and the lordly Tulip Tree, *Liriodendron tulipifera*, have been jealously guarded, and it is groves of these, or magnificent free-standing specimens, which make the bones of Winterthur, creating, with their noble height and maturity, the atmosphere of restful calm which is the chief attribute of the gardens.

But perhaps to the garden visitor who has no great horti-

RIGHT: *The white blossoms of azaleas floor the woods with snow*

The swimming pool in a setting of spring foliage and flowers

Low conifers grow in close mown lawn

cultural knowledge, but an eager eye, it is the choice of colours which will give the greatest pleasure: colour in all its gradations, in all its subtlety: brave, to bid 'the rash gazer wipe his eye', or soft

> Mid hush'd, cool-rooted flowers fragrant eyed,
> Blue, silver-white and budded Tyrian.

Save for one or two corners, the plan of the gardens at Winterthur is informal, so it is difficult to take the reader on a conducted tour, but several planting schemes deserve acclaim in fullest detail, so well do they illustrate the taste and wisdom in plant-lore of the gardens' creator. For instance, under a lofty canopy of Tulip trees, one of America's fairest native trees, with flowering Dogwood, *Cornus florida*, beneath them, are Kurume azaleas in many groups of separate colours. Below again grow all the lovely groundlings of spring, laying a carpet of pale colour, ferns, white three-petalled trilliums, anemones and blue and mauve scillas, violets and mertensias, with enchanting result.

At a safe distance, and quite out of sight of this garden, which a pre-Raphaelite, exchanging brush for spade, might well have planted, is a part of the garden with quite a different chiaroscuro – a massive group of *Rhododendron praevernum* in all its subtle tones of pink: with them, and more for their arresting glaucous foliage than for their flower, is planted *R. calophytum*. Nearby, but carefully chosen because their flowering season is later and so that their colours never coincide and clash, are some dark red azaleas, like Gable's Flame, Red Pippin and the blood red sport of Howraku which has been named Henry F. du Pont.

Clematis wreathes the stonework round a fountain

A canopy of green leaves shade a neatly architected flight of garden steps

This thoughtful arrangement works perfectly, for by the time the fiercer colours of the azaleas are ablaze, the more delicately shaded rhododendron flowers are over, and only their dark glossy leaves are left to act as a foil for the more strident colours of the shrubs whose flowering period follows.

Near here, grows a group of *Magnolia soulangeana*, called after the Chevalier Etienne Soulange-Bodin, a well-known French horticulturalist who lived in the early nineteenth century. This beautiful group of magnolias blossom at Winterthur in all their differing shades of white, pink and dark red. Beyond is a planting of which the predominating colour is white, achieving its greatest beauty in the month of May. Here are seen the pearly flowers of *Deutzia gracilis* and the Bridal Wreath *spiraeas*, with the pure flowers of *Azalea magnifica* covering a bank with snow: below a contrast is offered by a carpet of spring flowers such as golden jonquils – scillas – Star of Bethlehem in constellation, and the single spathed purple *Iris tectorum*, and the halcyon *Iris sibirica* to blend with the pure blue of the American native Quamash, *Camassia scilloides*, which raises its azure spires of flowers all about.

A little further and the colouring is all mauve, with the Kurume azaleas for which Winterthur is famous in a dozen variations of that subtle colour, to beautify the scene in early May. When they fade, the same shade is shown in lilacs in all their different tones of purple: lilacs such as *Syringa persica* with its delicate sprays of mauve headily-scented flowers in May, *laciniata* with smaller, but as sweet flowers, and *meyeri*, a lovely lilac from China, only introduced in 1923. Their colouring recalls the fact that Proust well named pigeons 'the lilacs of the feathered world'.

Blue is the predominant colour of the flowers which grow in the Sundial Garden, where the air is made spicy with the scent of *Phlox divaricata* and *P. stolonifera*, 'Blue Ridge', which are used as underplanting for wide bushes of the pale *chaenomeles* 'Apple Blossom', and more lilacs, including many of the old French varieties as well as the earlier-flowering *hyacinthiflora* types. The colour deepens, as this part of the garden merges into the next, and the splendid *Paulownia tomentosa* – which we see again at the Villa Taranto – shows its deep blue flowers, as do, nearby, the flowers of some deep purple azaleas such as Sherwood II, *mossianum* and *reticulatum*.

The variety of the colour schemes at Winterthur are infinite and a catalogue of names can grow tedious, but no memoir of the gardens would be complete without mention of the garden devoted entirely to Tree peonies. This garden, in its richness and number of plants is unique in the world, and is composed mostly of Professor Saunders' famous hybrids. Tree peonies

Trees and flowers as far as the eye can reach

Dogwood and spring foliage frame the Winterthur Museum in the background

Wide plantings of iris against a backdrop of evergreen and deciduous trees
A temple of white treillage in a glade of trees

Rhododendrons flower in the light shade cast by forest trees

were unknown in Europe, except in some oriental paintings, until the end of the eighteenth century, although they had long been the splendour and pride of monastery and palace gardens in China. First introduced in 1789 by Sir Joseph Banks, who gave his name to the beautiful banksian rose, their numbers were increased in the mid-nineteenth century by the wonderful plants sent from China by the celebrated plant collector Robert Fortune – lovely plants like Bijou de Chusan and Zenobia. The late Professor Arthur Percy Saunders (1869–1953), the great American botanist and hybridist, who for many years was the moving spirit of the American Peony Society, succeeded after much work and study in crossing the native *Peonia suffruticosa* with the yellow *Peonia lutea*, thus producing a completely new colour strain in peonies which now varies from golden yellow to terracotta. Professor Saunders' beautiful creations are to be seen at their best at Winterthur, and make a fine memorial to that great gardener's life work.

Seldom are the three gardening rules mentioned at the beginning of these notes – massive grouping, the preservation and utilization of existing trees and a meticulous blending of colour – so conscientiously carried out as at Winterthur. As the famous Museum, at whose doors the gardens lie, tells the story of the decorative arts of America in the early days of the Colonists so do the gardens exhibit American horticultural taste and science at their instructive best. The gardens have been endowed; they are now part of the American heritage, and so will delight many generations to come.

247

LEFT: *White Azalea mucronata alba line a walk through the pinetum*

Schloss Mainau LAKE CONSTANCE

The island-garden of a Swedish prince

'The Swedish Cross' which greets visitors to Schloss Mainau as they cross the causeway joining the island to the mainland. It is dated 1577

IN LAKE CONSTANCE, IN SOUTHERN GERMANY, lies an island which is all garden: the island of Mainau, named by the Knights of Reichenau and the Knights of the Teutonic Order *Maien-aue*, 'the Island of May Blossom'. Here Count Lennart Bernadotte, grandson of King Gustav of Sweden, has created a garden of unique beauty.

Count Bernadotte inherited the island from his grandmother, Queen Victoria of Sweden, who was born a Princess of Baden, within the borders of which state the island of Mainau lies. The island itself is quite small, less than a mile across at its greatest extent. In the thirteenth century it was bequeathed by Arnold of Langenstein to the Teutonic Knights and in 1271 the Prebend Mainau was founded on the island which already enjoyed a high reputation as 'a place of refuge and solace'. In 1740 the baroque castle which still crowns the island was built. By the Treaty of Pressburg in 1805 the island had passed to the Electors of Baden, in whose family it intermittently remained, until it became the property of the present owner.

The earliest owner of Mainau, of the Baden family, was Grand Duke Frederick I, who, early in the last century, and in the sentimental manner of the time, planted trees in memory of old friends, and had boulders carved with elevating verses. His great-grandson, Count Bernadotte, while preserving much of Grand Duke Frederick's features, has given the garden at Mainau new life and vitality, by the lavish planting of flowers and rare shrubs in the most brilliant colours. Thus a successful synthesis has been achieved, of nineteenth-century sentiment and twentieth-century botanical knowledge and gardening good taste. The first planter of the garden, 150 years ago, introduced many rare trees from other countries to Mainau. Many came from Kew, near London: cedars of Lebanon were introduced and one or two specimens of gingko, the Maiden-hair tree, which now tower a hundred and more feet high: as well as these, he introduced some giant sequoias from California, and there is a newly planted avenue of the lately discovered *Metase-*

RIGHT: *Above beds of serried masses of tulips and narcissus for which Count Bernadotte's garden is famous, rises the tower of the chapel*

The chapel tower looming over the sunlit leaves of a giant gunnera

A variety of
gardening styles
at the island
garden of Mainau

A crowned gryphon looks over the miniature harbour below the baroque Schloss

LEFT: *Details such as these tell that Mainau's owner is an original and resourceful garden planner. A pavement and terrace wall fashioned from tree trunks*

CENTRE LEFT: *An elegant rococo fountain against a pebblework background. The rose-wreathed urn bears the cipher of Frederick, Grand Duke of Baden*

EXTREME LEFT: *In the greenhouses of Mainau, some of which are removed in summer, grow dracaenas and other semi-tropical plants*

'Vue de l'Isle de Mainau dans le Lac de Constance', Mainau in the eighteenth century

quoia glyptostroboides which for centuries were thought to be extinct, and were only found in 1945 in a remote part of China, North-East Szechuan, and re-introduced to cultivation.

In spring, the gardens at Mainau are ablaze with daffodils and a kaleidoscopic collection of tulips, many of the latter being raised and flowered for the first time in this garden. Later in the year, colour and scent is provided by the rose garden which lies below the castle terrace: in autumn dahlias (first introduced into Germany in 1804 and called after the Swedish botanist Andreas Dahl) in their thousands fill the flowerbeds.

But the extraordinary feature of the garden at Mainau, and what makes it unique, is the tropical garden, where in temporary greenhouses for protection in winter, orchids and hundreds of other exotic plants are grown. In May, and with the coming of spring, the houses are dismantled, and visitors to Mainau are startled by the sight of date palms and banana trees waving their leaves against the northern sky.

At Mainau Count Bernadotte has created a garden which is both extraordinary and beautiful. In his veins, through his mother, the Grand Duchess Marie of Russia, who was so well known in America, runs the blood of Peter the Great, the creator of St Petersburg and Peterhof. Through the Swedish Royal line he descends from the Empress Josephine, whose grand-daughter became Queen of Sweden. There would be something for both these two utterly different ancestors in the garden at Mainau: the gentle Josephine would have delighted in the rose garden, with all the myriad new roses which were unknown when she planted the first of all rose gardens at Malmaison. Peter, who always looked eagerly beyond the confines of his country, and welcomed ideas from abroad, would have applauded the questing spirit of Count Bernadotte in collecting and giving a home to plants from all over the world.

Grand Duke Frederick of Baden, who first planted the garden at Mainau

253

LEFT: *The groves of Mainau are richly carpeted with tulips in early summer*

Sissinghurst Castle KENT

A flower-garden in the remains of a Tudor castle

SISSINGHURST CASTLE WAS BUILT in the reign of Henry VIII. For four centuries its pink tower of Tudor brick has looked over the orchards and hop-gardens of Kent. Earlier, a far older house stood on the site, dating back to the twelfth century, the Sissinghurst or Saxingherste which figures in the Combwell Abbey Charters.

Of the Tudor house, a large and imposing building, only some small parts survive, the tower among them. The house was built by an unattractive character, a politician and statesman under several Tudor monarchs, Sir John Baker, known as 'Bloody Baker' from the ferocity with which he persecuted the Protestants under Mary Tudor. Though only part of the original house exists today, it was still standing in some magnificence in 1752, when Horace Walpole dined there, and described the great courtyard as 'perfect and very beautiful'. But when Walpole saw it, its days of splendour were numbered: in 1760 it was no longer used as a private dwelling, but as a prison for French prisoners-of-war, and an interesting drawing survives of the Castle at this time. Afterwards, the great house stood desolate for twenty years, and much of the fabric was destroyed and the bricks carted away for use elsewhere: it was used, in short, as a quarry. Only the long range of the entrance building, the tower, some walls and one corner of the great courtyard, perfect no longer, survived. What remained was used as a poor-house, then as farm buildings. It was a fortunate day for Sissinghurst when in 1930 it became a private house once more.

Through all its vicissitudes, it is reasonable to suppose that some sort of cultivation had gone on round the castle's walls; so the soil of the garden, confusingly known as Tunbridge Wells sand, though it is not sand at all but a crumbly loam over stiff clay, must certainly have been cultivated, off and on, for centuries. Perhaps this fact has played a part in winning for Sissinghurst Castle its reputation of having the most beautiful garden in England, though we are more inclined to give the credit to the planning, and planting-genius, respectively, of its owners. Lady Nicolson, better known as V. Sackville-West, poet, writer

The Priest's House, beyond which stretches the Weald of Kent. At the foot of the house lies the white garden with its trim box hedges

LEFT: *The tower beyond the yew walk, and apple trees wreathed in roses*

The death and resurrection of a once palatial house

Sissinghurst was built in about 1550 as the country mansion of a Tudor statesman. The house was formed around three courtyards, the first of which survived while the second and third have almost entirely disappeared. During the Seven Years' War (1756-63) Sissinghurst was leased to the government as a prison for captured Frenchmen (RIGHT)

In the next 170 years the castle became almost completely derelict, and when the air-view (BELOW) was taken in 1932 there were only vegetable gardens

RIGHT: *An Alan Chandler rose climbs over the entrance archway*

SISSINGHURST

and gardener, gives Sir Harold full credit for the planning of the garden, though it was she who chose the plants and devised the planting schemes which imbue Sissinghurst with its special magic: 'I had the smaller part. Harold Nicolson did the designing, and I did the planting. We made a good combination in this way: I could not possibly have drawn out the architectural lines of the garden, and he couldn't possibly have planted it up, because he doesn't know quite as much about plants as I do. This is not saying much, for I know very little, but he knows even less. But he does know how to draw the axis between one view point and another, and that is something I could never have accomplished. To sum up, I think I have succeeded in making the garden pretty with my flowers, but the real credit it due to him, who drew its lines so well and so firmly that it can still be regarded with pleasure even in the winter months when all my flowers have vanished away, and the skeleton is revealed.'

It is the skeleton of the garden at Sissinghurst which rewards a gardener's study. The site, though full of possibilities, was not an easy one. There was little to go on; there were not, as might have been expected, any old trees: but there was the splendid tower, there were walls of rosy brick and there was the moat. But they were all at odd angles: the tower, for example, was not opposite the main entrance, and the courtyard was not square. But each was used to advantage and woven into the general plan. It was

A seat in the herb-garden

The lime-walk, in which are found many of the finest spring flowers

at this that Sir Harold excelled, as adept with pencil and squared paper as he is with his writer's pen. The result of his manipulation is entirely successful: the garden combines, in a most pleasing way, the qualities of formality of design with informality of planting. Long views have been conjured in a comparatively small area, the garden has been made to appear much larger than it is. The eye is constantly invited down some pleasing vista, and rewarded with the glimpse of a statue, a graceful seat or an opening between high yew hedges.

In the first three years, the Nicolsons planned, and did much hard work, with little hired labour, clearing the debris of centuries and all-possessive weeds from the area that was to be the garden. Of this period Miss Sackville-West has written: 'It was not until 1933 that any serious planting could be undertaken, but this was perhaps as well, because during those three impatient years we had time to become familiar with the "feel" of the place – a very important advantage which the professional garden-designer, abruptly called in, is seldom able to enjoy. A hundred times we changed our minds, but as we changed them only on paper, no harm was done and no expense incurred. Of course, we longed to start planting the hedges which were to be the skeleton of the garden, its bones, its anatomy, but had we been able to do so in those early days I am sure we should have planted them in the wrong place.'

How few were the mistakes they made can be seen by any visitor to Sissinghurst today. It is an easier garden than most to describe (though difficult to describe well) because its plan is so definite, and it can be visited, like a house, room by room. This was the original idea, 'that the garden with all its separate rooms and sub-sections must be a garden of seasonal features throughout the year; it was large enough to afford the space; we could have a spring garden, March to mid-May; and an early-summer garden, May-July; and a late-summer garden, July-August; and an autumn garden, September-October. Winter must take care of itself, with a few winter-flowering shrubs and some early bulbs.'

To enter the garden, the visitor passes through an arch of Tudor brick into the first courtyard. Rosemary laps the paved path and two great Irish yews rear blue-green pinnacles on either side. All round are walls of faded red brick, wreathed and looped with roses, powdery blue ceanothus and vines. An arch under the great tower leads to a further lawn, down a flight of steps, between tall classical vases. To the right, past a wall smothered with pink Albertine roses, with their coral buds, lies a path, balustered in box, to a doorway leading to the rose-garden. To the left, is another doorway in a brick wall, giving on to the white garden; this we will visit later.

Of the rose-garden V. Sackville-West has written: 'But I think my deepest stab of pleasure came when I discovered that the country people gave the name of Rondel to a circular patch

The Rondel, formed by yew hedges in the centre of the rose garden, seen from the top of the tower. The garden-wall was the back wall of one wing of the original house, and a doorway and window are preserved in it

of turf surrounded by one of our Yew hedges. There was all poetry, all romance, in that name; it suggested Provence and the troubadours and the Courts of Love; but I think I liked it even better when I realized that they were using it as a term far more Kentishly familiar to them: the name they normally gave to the round floor for drying hops inside one of our Kentish oasts.'

The 'Rondel' is now surrounded by high yew hedges, with old roses behind which are at their glorious, but short-lived, best in June: but their short flowering period is compensated by an interplanting of iris, peonies, the tall lemon-coloured spires of Eremurus, and white belled Yuccas: all these have either a background of brick wall or darkling yew.

Of this particular part of the garden Miss Sackville-West has written: 'This in former days would almost automatically have become a herbaceous border, very garish in July and August, and far more pleasing no doubt to the general public, but to my mind the shrubs available today (many of which were of course unknown to our grandparents) are more interesting as well as more saving of labour.' This is excellent garden-sense and sums up modern ideas on decorative gardening.

A path through the rose-garden leads to a pleached lime walk, with a roughly paved path planted on either side with all the early flowers of the year. This is a part of the Sissinghurst garden which comes to its greatest beauty in spring: here grow all the delicate groundlings whose fragile beauty is the more moving because they flower so soon after the rough cold of winter: blue anemones, scillas and chionodoxas, with the earliest iris and species tulips and Dog Tooth Violets. The picture they present might be the detail of a Botticelli. At one end of this walk, brooding over the carpet of misty colour laid at her feet is a gracefully draped statue. At the other end is a nut-wood, underplanted with polyanthus to make a multicoloured mosaic of colour in May. On one side azaleas blaze in June, alongside the moat walk, walled on one side only. This leads to the herb-garden, where grow many herbs other than the usual thyme, fennel and tarragon; herbs such as woad, once grown by the ancient British inhabitants of Kent for sartorial purposes, as it supplied the blue dye with which they painted their naked hides: at Sissinghurst *Isatis tinctoria* is grown for its attractive habit and yellow flowers. The paths in the herb-garden are carpeted with mats of different thymes, as Bacon counselled in his famous essay *Of Gardens*: 'Therefor you are to set whole alleys of them, to have the pleasure when you walk or tread': but at Sissinghurst herbs are used for two further purposes, and less usual ones: a stone bench has a cushioned seat of herbs, a revival of an old Elizabethan practice: the other is an original invention of V. Sackville-West herself. 'Just outside the herb-garden I thought it might be suitable to have a lawn of thyme. This was one of my successes, and I invented it, so far as I know, as my own idea. I had never seen it anywhere else, nor had I

A statue sheltered by a silver-leaved willow

LEFT: *The tower seen from a corner of the South Cottage garden*

SISSINGHURST

A statue of Dionysus reflected in the moat

The garden of the South Cottage

read about it. It was cheap and quick and easy to produce: we just tore to pieces some of the *Thymus serpyllum* already growing in paved paths, and dibbled them in, and within a year the little beds were dense. It really looks pretty when in flower, red and purple, and it looks tidy and green for the rest of the year, and as it flowers at the same time as the *Iris sibirica* behind it, with the dark water of the moat beyond, it makes a separate picture for at least six weeks.'

Leaving the moat, we approach the castle once more. Regaining the tower lawn we turn right and make our way to the white garden by the Priest's House. This, to many, and to the compiler of this book certainly, is the most beautiful of all the gardens at Sissinghurst, and indeed of anywhere in England. It has its greatest magic in June, when cloudy with white roses growing through almond trees, and with its air laden with the incense of white Regale lilies, their flowers, it seems, afloat on a mist of gypsophila and silver-leaved plants. It is a garden that is cool and fresh and deliciously scented. A garden to dream in, and of.

One other garden is still unvisited – the cottage garden which lies in front of the little house, relic of the castle, where Harold Nicolson writes in a room with lead-paned windows, and rosemary growing, literally, out of the window-sill. The colours here are warm and welcoming and the garden is paved in a happy mixture of paving stones and old bricks. In the centre stands a copper, green with age: all around are flowers in shades of orange, yellow and red – roses, columbines, geums, and peonies. A Mme Alfred Carrière rose clothes the cottage to its eaves; nearby roses, whose roots Miss Sackville-West brought from Persia, now revel in the Kentish loam. Here yellow peonies loll at the path side, bedfellows to yellow tulips and velvet pansies; and a golden canary creeper comes to rest on cushions of ginger-coloured rock roses. The garden is untidy – but with a controlled untidiness. The planting looks as if it had all just happened, like a real cottage garden: it is all as human and intimate as a secret.

The cottage garden, and the whole garden at Sissinghurst offer examples of modern garden-planting at its most brilliant: only a gardener with the eye of an artist, and an artist with a gardener's fingers, could have created them. Again and again at Sissinghurst it is apparent to the observant visitor that its planners have worked to a definite rule: to create a garden full of flowers and colour, full to overflowing, but not quite overflowing its lineal plan. How closely that rule has been followed, and how transcendingly successful the result, any visitor to Sissinghurst will see. The garden is open to the public every day from May to October, and Miss Sackville-West's heirs have maintained it exactly as she would have wished.

Miss Sackville-West died at Sissinghurst on June 2nd, 1962. The photographs which accompany this description were taken a few days after her death.

RIGHT: *An archway in the rose garden*

Villa Taranto LAKE MAGGIORE

A Scotsman's magnificent collection of shrubs

A bronze fisherboy by Gemito near the swimming pool, cleverly contrived to blend into the terraced garden

PROBABLY THE LARGEST GARDEN in the world still in private occupation, the gardens of the Villa Taranto spread their hundred acres on the northern banks of Lake Maggiore. They have been brought to their present perfection in far less than a lifetime, for they were not planted until as recently as 1930. The owner, Captain Neil McEacharn, came on the site, almost by chance, while driving from Venice to London, and at once seized on its possibilities, though to a less perceptive eye these might not have been so apparent. Though the setting was superb, with the lake washing the lower slopes of the property and with the towering Alps beyond, the garden itself was utterly undistinguished, and no effort had been made to make anything of it; thus the project of making a garden there not only offered great interest, but a certain challenge as well.

Captain McEacharn, an experienced and knowledgeable gardener, had long entertained a secret ambition to plan a garden in the English style, in some climate kinder than that of his native Scotland, and to plant it with as many exotic and delicate shrubs as could be assembled from all over the world. The Taranto site seemed to provide the ideal conditions for such an interesting project – sheltered by the Alps, bathed in the Italian sun, and with abundant water at hand from the lake.

First a new landscape had to be conjured. The physical con-

LEFT: *The lotus pool with steps inspired by a garden in Portugal*

Natural planting and formality at Taranto

White tulips with the spray of the cherub fountain beyond

LEFT: *The valley garden provides shelter for many rare plants*

267

VILLA TARANTO

A pergola hung with the mauve racemes of wisteria

tours of the site were re-sculpted into their present smooth and undulating shape. Few visitors to the gardens of the Villa Taranto today would believe what changes have been made to achieve the new, but entirely natural-seeming, lie of the land. The present gentle slopes look as if they have been there for centuries.

The dark, friable, lime-free soil of the garden offers lush nourishment for every sort of plant, while the rise and fall of the ground provides endless scope for dramatic planting. Captain McEacharn has adhered closely to his original plan, and profited, thirty years ago when the work was first started, by the cheap labour then available, to build miles of roads and paths as well as terraces, culverts and retaining walls to support his newly created slopes. Without this solid construction the overwhelming rains of the *Temporale*, the sudden storm which can lash Lake Maggiore, might have washed away soil and plants in a few hours. To prevent this, great blocks of rough local granite from the quarries of Fondo Toce were used to strengthen the newly created landscape.

The house, white and cool, with the elegant air of a small French château of the Midi, stands at the end of the estate furthest away from the lake, as if at the point of a V, with the gardens growing wider as they stretch towards the water. From the terrace, steps descend to one of the many English features of the garden – a fresh wide lawn of a quality seldom found in Italy. Its brilliant green expanse is broken only by a central fountain, tossing its water high into the air. Beyond lie the gardens, with their miles of paths, brimming borders and groves of high trees sheltering delicate shrubs below.

A plant much grown at Villa Taranto, which is rather an exotic in Italy, is the rhododendron – and these always excite interest and curiosity in Italian visitors. Though they do not prosper in Italy as they do at Bodnant in Wales, or around the lake at Stourhead, many thrive at Villa Taranto, though they miss the humidity and the more constant temperature of Britain. Two that grow well, however, are the large exotic-leaved *Rhododendron sinogrande*, which came to Lake Maggiore from China by way of Captain McEacharn's garden in Scotland, and the yellow-belled *R. falconeri*.

Magnolias are one of the sights of the garden in spring, especially *Magnolia stellata*, the starry magnolia of English gardens, with its narrow petalled snowy flowers in March. Captain McEacharn also grows the far rarer pink variety, which he found in Holland in 1932. Another magnolia which takes the eye in spring with its sensational crimson cup-flowers vivid against the blue Italian sky, is *Magnolia campbelli*. But rarities are commonplace in the garden of the Villa Taranto; for instance, in a sheltered part of the garden called the Valley there is a grove of bananas, *Musa basjoo*, with enormous leaves shaped like the sails of a Chinese junk. Nearby grow paulownias, named

RIGHT : *The cherub fountain at the Villa Taranto seen below the flower-laden branches of paulownia*

VILLA TARANTO

A bouquet of palm trees, the graceful Trachycarpus Fortunei, beyond a moon-shaped pool

after a daughter of the Czar Paul of Russia, Anna Paulowna, who became Queen of Holland. They were first grown in England in 1840. At Villa Taranto they seed freely and their lovely pale blue flowers, like the flower spires, in shape and colour, of hyacinths, are a glory in April, before their great heart-shaped velvety leaves unfold. The seldom grown *Paulownia fortunei* is one of the prizes of Taranto. It came as a seedling from Kew in 1934, and took fourteen years to flower, though it has done so ever since; today the trees are thirty feet high, and when in flower, they lay a delicious scent of carnations on the air around them.

Other plants which are Captain McEacharn's especial pride, include *chaenomeles*, of which there is a distinguished collection at Villa Taranto, in all their brilliant colouring of pink-salmon, apricot and deeper crimsons and scarlets. These shrubs make flower-covered, spreading trees and remain in beauty over a long period, thus living up to their Japanese name 'Flower of a Hundred Days'. Many, in fact, came from Wada's famous nursery in Japan.

America, too, has supplied many of the loveliest trees at Villa Taranto, among them that loveliest of American natives, the dogwood, *Cornus florida rubra*, which brightens the scene in spring with its rosy flowers; many came from the Andorra nurseries in Philadelphia in 1935.

Although the attractions of the gardens at Villa Taranto are numberless, one in particular lures the visitor with a curious spell, the lotus pool. Here a flight of steps, designed like some that Captain McEacharn saw in a garden in Portugal, descend to the water, in which grow the rose-coloured flowers of *Nelumbo nucifera*, each chiselled flower held proudly above a forest of circular leaves of lacquered green which recall the design on an Oriental screen. Other exotic water plants to be seen are the Amazonian water-lily *Victoria amazonica* and *Victoria crusiana*, which are grown under glass. Their great circular leaves measure seven feet across and their exquisite pink flowers, though each one only lasts for twenty-four hours or less, are born in great profusion. These rare water-lilies come from the upper stretches of the Amazon, and are grown almost nowhere else in Europe.

Lotus have long been grown in Italy, as visitors to Stra near Venice will recall, but it is important to remember that the vast majority, nearly ninety per cent, of the flowers and trees grown at the Villa Taranto were never grown in Italy at all until Captain McEacharn introduced them. This reason alone gives the gardens great importance. Another is the Villa Taranto Seed Catalogue, known and eagerly looked for every year by garden connoisseurs all over the world. This catalogue, which lists seeds available from the gardens at Villa Taranto, goes out not only to private garden-owners of standing, but to botanical gardens everywhere: thus, seed of the botanical treasures of Taranto is spread far and wide. In 1936, when the first catalogue

In its setting of rare trees and shrubs, the cool Villa Taranto has a French air

The flowers of the magnificent Paulownia imperialis scent the air for yards around

was prepared there were only 367 names listed: today there are over four thousand.

It has been written:

These then are the gardens of the Villa Taranto, formal yet natural, rare and exotic without obvious artificiality, vigorous and transcendental without obtrusive debt either to art or to nature. So composite a creation contrived in a period so relatively short – despite the intervention of the war with its consequent difficulties and the absence of Captain McEacharn for six years – witnesses the great passion, the unceasing care, the unaltered perseverance with which its owner has pursued his aim.

The future of the gardens is assured. Over twenty years ago Captain McEacharn expressed the hope that the gardens on his death should be maintained as an Italian equivalent of the famous Kew Botanical Gardens in England. This hope has been gratefully acknowledged by the Italian Government, which in the name of the Italian nation, has accepted the gift of the gardens.

Keukenhof HOLLAND

A natural garden in the land of bulbs

BETWEEN THE HAGUE AND HARLEM lies flat sandy countryside, over which, five hundred years ago, might have been seen a gaily dressed cavalcade of men and women out hawking. They would have looked, under the immense sky of Holland, like a picture by Wouverman or Paul Potter, as they galloped over the sand-dunes, led possibly by a mannish looking young woman of thirty, Jacqueline of Hainault. In her short life of thirty-five years, Jacqueline was married three times; first, at the age of fourteen, to the French Duc de Berri, who died soon afterwards; then to her close relation, the Duke Jan van Brabant. This union shocked her family, who accused her of incest and forced her to ask the Pope for an annulment. Her last attempt at matrimony was with Duke Humphrey of Gloucester, brother of King Henry V of England. Duke Humphrey, though a hero of Agincourt, proved a most unsatisfactory husband; once he had possessed himself of Jacqueline's estates and fortune, he was openly unfaithful to her with one of her ladies-in-waiting, Eleanor Cobham (whom he afterwards married), and so caused her to retire indignantly to her castle at Teylingen. Thenceforward, embittered and yet still young and active, Jacqueline found an outlet for her energies in the pursuit of falconry on her nearby estate of Keukenhof.

Jacqueline's hunting grounds became, five hundred years later, a world-famous garden.

The modern garden of Keukenhof lies between the two great modern roads that link The Hague and Harlem, near the village of Lisse. A few miles only from the coast, it is sheltered from the winds of the North Sea by high sand-dunes. The soil is calciferous and sandy, and the level of the ground is seldom more than 0·70 to 3·00 metres above the normal water-table – ideal conditions for growing bulbs.

The story of how the garden came into being is a short one. In 1949, when the estate of Keukenhof, for years the country seat of the distinguished family of Van Lynden, had become, owing to changing conditions, difficult to maintain, the enterprising bulb-growers of Holland saw a magnificent opportunity of

The earliest known picture of a tulip, from Konrad Gesner's 'De Hortis Germaniae Liber', 1561

LEFT: *Tulips at the Keukenhof, with hyacinths and daffodils beyond*

Crown Imperials by the waterside

Narcissus by the lake

putting into effect a long-cherished idea. They entered into a ten-year agreement (since extended to twenty years) with the owner of the estate, and after obtaining a financial guarantee from the surrounding municipal councils, they set about creating a great bulb-park. By the spring of 1950 over fifty acres of the neglected woodland had been cleared. Dead trees were removed; marshes were turned into lawns; ditches were filled in; ugly patches were re-modelled; stagnant ponds were conjured into lucent pools. In 1951 the park area grew to over sixty acres. There were eight miles of paths, and fine air-conditioned and heat-controlled greenhouses were added to produce a magnificent display of indoor tulips in all their infinite varieties.

By 1953 the Keukenhof had expanded still more. Its park area was now seventy-five acres, the paths had grown to fifteen miles, and many other amenities had been added to make it the delight of the million people who visited it. Every year now sees further growth, and more plans for new beauties and attractions, such as the inclusion of sculpture by outstanding young

RIGHT: *Numberless varieties of tulips are grown at the Keukenhof*

Tulips . . . Holland's
own flower, grown in
the greatest bulb-
garden in the world

The old castle

Princess Jacqueline of Hainault, 1401–36. A fifteenth-century portrait painted on wood in the Rijksmuseum

modern artists. The Keukenhof now contains nearly a hundred different gardens, displaying the latest and best of the leading bulb-growers of Holland. Each has a character and design of its own; each has a different setting and appeal. Some specialize in great collections of perfect tulips and hyacinths and other flowers grown from bulbs, some in massive beds of one colour, 'to make the rash gazer wipe his eye'. Others present almost the whole family of narcissus; and one magnificent sight is the wonderful 200-yard avenue of ancient beech trees under which grow hundreds of thousands of daffodils, producing a vista of waving gold and orange and cream and green unequalled in the world. Groups of variegated tulips demonstrate that nature's colours never clash, no matter how prodigally they are scattered. The colours at Keukenhof are truly kaleidoscopic – a carpet of azure *muscari* under the silver-barked birches, tulips as stiff-backed and scarlet as London guardsmen, or striped like a troubadour's hose by the lake's edge, and hyacinths in softer subtler colours to seduce the eye and lay their heady scent on the ambient air.

A work by British sculptor, Barbara Hepworth, in the garden at Keukenhof

KEUKENHOF

The flowers of the Keukenhof attract many thousands of tourists every year. In 1957, in gratitude for providing such an outstanding attraction for American visitors to Holland, the Holland America Shipping Company bought, restored and offered as an embellishment to the grounds of Keukenhof a fine old Gröningen windmill, which now stands in one corner of the garden, its sails casting slow-moving shadows on the flowers beneath. Nearby is the lake, and on it float many kinds of duck, dappled Shelldrakes, Gadwalls and Garganeys; and now and then glide past, aloof and majestic, the exotic black-necked swans from Brazil for which the Keukenhof is famous.

Plans are afoot to extend the season of interest of the gardens beyond the spring and early summer months by planting trees and shrubs which flower later in the year and provide autumn colour. So, soon, the yearly number of visitors to this splendid well-ordered Dutch garden, unique in its size and the spectacle it offers, will grow from the quarter of a million who visited it in 1950 to well past the 803,000 who came in 1967.

The filigree of young beech leaves

RIGHT: '*Nature's colours never clash*'

Savill Gardens WINDSOR

The gardens in the royal park

The young foliage of spring in the Savill garden

ENGLAND HAS MANY MAGNIFICENT LANDSCAPE GARDENS; some are still kept up, though not as they were in the Edwardian heyday of unlimited and inexpensive labour, but many others have disappeared. These great gardens of the past were conjured by the wealth and horticultural enthusiasm of private individuals. But the woodland gardens at Windsor are different; they have been created by the vision of a few keen gardeners, the Deputy Ranger of Windsor Park, Sir Eric Savill in particular, and financed in part by public funds, but also by generous gifts from the gardening public; and the whole concept has been encouraged by the support of the Royal Family. In fact, it is fair to say that but for the interest of King George V and Queen Mary, and later the even more personal part played in the creation of the gardens by King George VI and Queen Elizabeth, the Gardens at Windsor would never have been: but they are in no sense private Royal Gardens. They are visited by thousands of visitors every year, and by garden connoisseurs from all over the world.

Natural gardens, which is what the Windsor Gardens *in excelsis* are, are a particularly English concept. America, with its cypress gardens and camellia gardens in the South, is almost the only other country to have planted them. A natural garden, in the simplest terms, is an area already embellished with mature trees, where suitable plants are set, and then left to look after themselves – rhododendrons in woodland, for instance, or primulas by the side of a stream. For a natural garden, therefore, site is all-important, and in planning the gardens at Windsor the greatest care was given to its selection. Mr Lanning Roper, in his excellent book, *The Gardens in the Royal Park at Windsor*, writes:

> There were many factors to be considered – satisfactory soil, natural shelter from wind for tender plants, freedom from damage from late frost, adequate moisture and a high shade canopy for woodland plants. Water, either in streams or ponds, preferably in both, was highly desirable.

Visitors to the Windsor Gardens today, only thirty years after their first planting, will soon see with what skill the site was

RIGHT: *White rhododendrons under a high canopy of trees*

originally chosen. Most of the part of the park chosen for the gardens was used merely as cover for the game for which Windsor Great Park was famous, a thick tangle of laurels, stunted oaks, elders and bracken. The ordinary *Rhododendron ponticum* proliferated like weeds and spread for acres, delighting in the acid soil which all their genus demands. All this needed much labour to clear, and as the work progressed, the beauties of the site became apparent. Streams were dammed to make ponds, and the ancient silver-boled beeches of Windsor, under which the Plantagenet, Tudor and Stuart kings had hunted, stood out in all their majesty. Long rides were cut through thickets of undergrowth which may once have echoed to the ghostly horn of Herne the Hunter. As the trees were thinned, more blue sky showed overhead, and in turn was reflected in the newly-formed ponds and streams. Where trees are cut, primroses and bluebells, as if by magic always appear, and so, without a single flower being planted, the woodland became a garden. Soon, of course, other flowers, flowering shrubs and trees were afterwards planted in thousands. Rhododendrons were naturally first choice, as the soil at Windsor is so perfectly suited to them. Others were magnolias (many of the rarer kinds are now just reaching their flowering age), eucryphias, camellias, lilies and primulas, but though a fine start had been made, the gardens (this was in the early 'thirties) had far from reached their full development and room was still needed for the more ambitious plans of the Deputy Ranger.

The turning point of the enterprise came when King George and Queen Mary visited what is now known as the Savill Garden, the far larger Valley Garden being laid out much later. The visit, it is related, began badly, for a branch caught in Queen Mary's toque and nearly disarranged it. Soon, however, things improved. The massive work which had already been done made its impression, and the imagination and enthusiasm of the royal pair was kindled: as they left, delighted with their visit, the Queen said that the new garden was very nice, but was it not, surely, a little small? 'This,' says Lanning Roper 'was the longed-for accolade. This was the green light.' And ever since that day, in spite of the war and ever-changing conditions work on the gardens has gone forward.

Today the gardens at Windsor have reached maturity, and for at least eight months of the year present a picture of great beauty. Even in winter, a visit to the garden is rewarding, if only for the sculptural grace of the trees, and the flash of crimson of the pollarded dogwood; and there is, at Windsor, an unusual garden-within-a-garden, in which only flowers and shrubs which can be expected to flower on Christmas Day, are planted. Of the two gardens at Windsor, the first to be cleared and planted was the smaller and more intimate Savill garden, called after Sir Eric Savill, deputy ranger of Windsor Great Park, ever the moving spirit of the enterprise. Here, down a glade canopied

Lilium giganteum *in the Savill garden*

LEFT: *White rhododendron of the scented Loderi group*

285

Daffodils star the turf under one of the old oaks of Windsor

Lysichitum americanum, *the skunk cabbage with its luxurious leaves*

with trees, runs a stream with its either bank planted with iris, the pink *Primula rosea* and the golden *P. prolifera*, interspersed with bold clumps of the American skunk cabbage, *Lysichitum americanum*, with its luxurious leaves and huge arum lilies of flowers. All around stand great beech trees and oaks, and in the dappled shades they cast grow rare rhododendrons like *R. souliei*, known as the Windsor Park variety, recognized as one of the loveliest of all rhododendrons.

Then there is the far larger Valley garden, over 200 acres in extent which has been laid out since the war and is still being greatly developed. This stretches as far as Virginia Water and offers conditions which are specially suitable for the flowering of the large leaved Asiatic rhododendrons which were the great interest and love of the late King George VI. It is here that are planted many rare species of rhododendron from the celebrated Stevenson collection at Tower Court, Ascot.

To the south-east of the Valley Gardens, lies almost the most spectacular garden of all – the Kurume Punchbowl. Here is a large, natural amphitheatre, which has been planted with massed azaleas in enormous groups in all their different colours; the garden presents a brilliant palette of crimson, scarlet and pink for weeks on end every summer. The Punchbowl is one of the garden sights of England every year.

What are the other features of the Windsor gardens? The herbaceous border, 35 feet wide, so large enough to include shrubs and the shrub roses, such as the heraldic-looking *Rosa moyesii*, tamarisks and foaming lilacs, which give body and architectural form to the borders even when they are not in full flower: while

Reflections in a flower-framed pool of the Savill garden

nearby, in June, there is a garden full of the old roses which have found new favour, and in high summer the air there is heavy with the scent of roses whose very name breathes romantic fancy, roses with names like *Cuisse de Nymphe émue*, and names that whisper history, like *Châpeau de Napoleon* with buds recalling the Emperor's hat, and *Deuil du Roi de Rome*. Last, in this record of the delights of the Savill and Valley Gardens, but to some almost the most fascinating of all, is the garden protected by the great wall built in 1951, which forms the north boundary of the Savill Garden; 18 feet high and sturdily buttressed, this wall was built out of old bricks salvaged from bombed buildings in London, and in its protection grow tender and rare shrubs and climbers; alongside it are raised scree beds for cushiony alpines and more rare and delicate plants. Of this beautiful and peaceful corner of the Savill Garden, Lanning Roper has truly said 'Here beauty and life have become the by-products of destruction and death.'

In conclusion, I quote what Dr Harold Fletcher, Regius Keeper of the Royal Botanic Gardens, Edinburgh, has said of the Gardens at Windsor:

In 1931 there was not a garden in the whole of the Great Park at Windsor. Today there are great and lovely plantings, over 200 acres in extent, of a magnificent range of ornamental plants from all parts of the temperate regions of the world. These give abiding pleasure to the lover of flowers and of trees and shrubs, as well as to the botanist. I think it is quite true to say that no other garden with which I am familiar so beautifully and efficiently integrates the wide interests of horticulturists, aboriculturists and botanists – and this, it seems to me, is the great significance of the Windsor Gardens.

There is a fine collection of 'old-fashioned' and species roses at Windsor: Rosa bourboniana, '*Zigeuner knabe*', *with rich purple flowers*

A note on the photographs

The author and publishers are grateful to the owners of the gardens illustrated in this book for permission to photograph them and for their help in many other ways.

The following photographers took the photographs of the gardens mentioned against their names:

EDWIN SMITH: La Gamberaia; Villandry; Levens Hall; The Vatican Garden; Bomarzo; Vaux-le-Vicomte;. Versailles; Villa Garzoni, Collodi; Chatsworth; Stourhead; Courances; The Nymphenburg; Bagatelle; Marlia; Tresco Abbey; Bodnant; Hidcote Manor; Villa Taranto; Savill

KERRY DUNDAS: Kasteel Twickel; Earlshall; Schwetzingen; Veitshöchheim; Powerscourt; Schloss Mainau; Keukenhof

GERTI DEUTSCH: Alhambra; Aranjuez; Fronteira

GOTTSCHO-SCHLEISNER: Williamsburg; Charleston; Old Westbury; Winterthur

GURINENKO and JOHN DAYTON: Peterhof

Each chapter is also illustrated by certain additional pictures. We are grateful to Mrs Judy Blofeld for her assistance in obtaining these extra illustrations; and to the following persons or institutions for permission to reproduce them, or for other help in connection with those particular gardens:

Alhambra: Marquesa de Casa Valdes, Professor F. Prieto-Moreno, Library RIBA, Kerry Dundas

La Gamberaia: Doctor Marcello Marchi, Peter Coats

Kasteel Twickel: Miss Cremers

Aranjuez: Marquesa de Casa Valdes, Africa House

The Vatican Garden: Kerry Dundas, Peter Coats

Vaux-le-Vicomte: British Museum

Williamsburg: Colonial Williamsburg Photographs, Thomas L. Williams

Versailles: Witt Library of the Courtauld Institute of Art, Bulloz (Paris)

Peterhof: Mr and Mrs Victor Kennett, Department of Fine Arts of the Ministry of Culture for the Preservation of Monuments in the USSR, N. I. Arhipov, A. G. Raskin, Christopher Marsden

Fronteira: The Duchess of Palmella

Schwetzingen: Herr Kurt Martin

Chatsworth: Francis Thompson, Thomas Wragg, The Trustees of the Chatsworth Settlement, Airviews Ltd

Stourhead: The National Trust, British Museum

Veitshöchheim: Curator of Veitshöchheim, Peter Coats, Nicholas Powell

Courances: Le Vicomte de Noailles, M. le Marquis de Ganay

The Nymphenburg: Museum at Schloss Nymphenburg, Aero Express München

Bagatelle: The Wallace Collection, The Metropolitan Museum of Art Rogers Fund 1922

Marlia: Count Pecci Blunt

Charleston: Frick Art Reference Library, J. E. Downward, Kerry Dundas

Tresco Abbey: The Royal Horticultural Society Journal

Powerscourt: Christopher Hussey

Bodnant: G. E. Lloyd

The Huntington Botanical Gardens: Wendland, Francis Reinhart, Gabi Roma, Henry E. Huntington Library and Art Gallery

Hidcote Manor: The National Trust, J. E. Downward, Peter Coats

Winterthur: Gilbert Ask

Schloss Mainau: Countess Cecilie Bernadotte, Herr Raft, Herr Pröpstl

Villa Taranto: Kerry Dundas

Keukenhof: The Dutch Bulb Growers Association, F. Doerflinger, Rijksmuseum, Amsterdam, Peter Coats

Savill Gardens: Sir Eric Savill, Lanning Roper, J. E. Downward, Peter Coats

Endpapers: The National Trust

The author is particularly grateful to Lanning Roper and Joan Parry Dutton for their advice on the gardens in the United States of America; to His Excellency the German Ambassador for his help with the German gardens; to P. Stageman of the Royal Horticultural Society Library